SUDOC 18

THE BARN

LIFE IN HOLLAND DURING THE NAZI
OCCUPATION OF THE SECOND WORLD WAR

*A Family Memoir transcribed,
edited & annotated by Jack Dixon*

Copyright © 2014 by Jack Dixon
First Edition – August 2014

ISBN
978-1-4602-3968-1 (Hardcover)
978-1-4602-3969-8 (Paperback)
978-1-4602-3970-4 (eBook)

All rights reserved.

No part of this publication may be reproduced in any form, or by any means, electronic or mechanical, including photocopying, recording, or any information browsing, storage, or retrieval system, without permission in writing from the publisher.

Produced by:

FriesenPress
Suite 300 – 852 Fort Street
Victoria, BC, Canada V8W 1H8

www.friesenpress.com

Distributed to the trade by The Ingram Book Company

Table of Contents

1   Prelude: May 1940

21   Part One: Occupation: 1940 - 1944

87   Part Two: Evacuation

143   Part Three: Liberation

171   Postlude

179   Appendix A

183   Appendix B

ACKNOWLEDGEMENTS

This is the true story of one family involved in the horrors of the Nazi Occupation of their country in the Second World War. That country was The Netherlands, more popularly known as Holland. It is from the members of that family that I obtained by word of mouth the events narrated here. If there is one member of that family to whom I owe the most, I must not be shy in acknowledging that it is to the girl in the story called Ria. That girl is my wife.

I have been free to write it in my own words, but my words have faithfully recorded what happened, and I have not hesitated to explain why, in many instances. Where Ria's or others' memories have been a bit vague or uncertain, I have researched the events and people and places in question, and filled in the blanks in a way that can be shown to be historically accurate. One example is in the identity of the Canadian Army unit which actually liberated the town in which Ria and her family were living at the time.

I have added footnotes where necessary to explain details which would otherwise have remained obscure. And I have added two Appendixes: one elaborating on the evacuation of the entire civilian population of Arnhem and its surrounding towns and villages following the Allied defeat at the Battle of Arnhem in September 1944; the other an interview, on November 10, 2010, with one of the Canadian soldiers who actually took part in the liberation of the town where Ria and her family were living, on April 1-2, 1945. Due acknowledgement is made in the appropriate places.

We also wish to thank the Netherlands War Museum, and our friend Auke Wagenaar of Nijmegen, Holland, for researching most of the illustrations appearing here; and I thank my Project Manager at FriesenPress, Dana Mills, for her skills and patience.

DEDICATION

This book is dedicated to the brave people of Holland who, by their moral resistance to the enemy within their gates, made possible "the eventual transformation of Germany into a prosperous and dynamic democracy"; and most especially to one of those people, my beloved wife, Rika.

PRELUDE

MAY 1940

I.

She sat up in bed with a start. What was that noise? It was still distant, but it seemed like a heavy metallic clunking and a dull rumbling noise. She listened intently, and nervously, fearing the worst. It was something unknown to her, and threatening. There was that clanking again, now getting louder.

She was fully awake now, and out of bed, quickly but quietly, and despite the darkness, slipping on her robe as she made her way out of the bedroom and down the stairs. The noise was getting louder, and to it was added another noise...Oh, my Lord, it was shooting, the firing of guns. She went to the window of the front room, and there was her husband, looking out onto the street. She hadn't noticed his absence when she got up. But then he sensed her presence.

"It's the *moffen*!" he said, turning round, as calmly as he could. "The *moffen*[1] are here! First Poland, now us."

Mrs Mollen clung to her husband, seeking reassurance.

"But why?" she asked fearfully. "Why us? We are neutral."

"With maniacs like Hitler, who knows!"

"We will have to wake up the children."

"They'll wake up anyway.."

Mrs Mollen went to the door of the kitchen, then, changing her mind, went back upstairs to her bedroom. She happened to notice that the clock in the hall showed a few minutes after four.

---

1 A familiar term of disapproval or contempt for 'Germans'. Its origin is unknown.

Slowly, and sleepily, their children began to emerge from their rooms, and joined their parents downstairs. They explained to them what was happening as calmly as they could. The two older boys could not refrain from peering round the edges of the curtains. And what they saw confirmed their fears.

*   *   *

The German Army was marching past their house as they stormed through the town, troops with rifles, troops with machine guns, and especially tanks. Tanks! That is what was making the frightening, heavy metallic clanking noise.

The noise of shooting was heard again in the background. The youngest of the children, their daughter, Ria, looked round to her mother, wondering and apprehensive.

"What is that noise, Mama?"

"The Germans are shooting. I hope they are not shooting our soldiers or our people."

"Maybe our soldiers are shooting them?"

"I hope no one is getting shot."

"Are they going to kill us, Papa?"

"Of course not, child. We will make sure they don't harm you or your brothers and sisters."

After the tanks, the marching started—marching and stomping and shouting. Sergeants and Corporals marching beside the columns of troops, spurring them on, shouting at them all the time, shouting commands and threats and orders in that guttural, violent language of theirs.

INVASION

It was the shouting, penetrating through the doors and windows of their house and violating their privacy, that struck foreboding into them, as much as the tanks were the image of brutal power deployed against innocent and helpless people. It was the shouting, the ever-present invasive shouting, used as a calculated weapon of intimidation, that was going to become a grievous feature of the lives of their family, as of all Dutch families, for the next five years.

"Let us go and get dressed, children," said their mother. "There will be no more rest for us this night. Then we will have an early breakfast."

'Children', did we say? Well, it is a useful, collective term, though we were aged from twenty-two to eleven, and evenly spaced, as in most good Catholic families. The two oldest were boys, Gerrit and Rudy, in their early twenties. Then the oldest daughter, Ina, who was 18. Then came Jan, 16. And last but not least, Bert aged 14, and Ria, not quite 12. Then there was the oldest, Ennie, who was married and living in Amsterdam. But she takes no part in this story. We must not fail to mention Willie, the oldest, who was in the Dutch Army out in the Dutch East Indies somewhere. It had been some time since his last letter.

II.

An hour later, although it was still only six o'clock in the morning, the family reassembled in the family room, and Mr Mollen switched on the wireless.[2]

> ...that the German Army, without provocation, without a declaration of war, and contrary to international law, diplomatic protocol, or a decent concern for humanitarian principles, have trampled down our barriers, invaded our country, and at this very moment are surging forward across our land virtually without resistance. There has been some spirited opposition at the frontier posts. We understand that a few kilometres from Arnhem [all look at each other, at first frightened, then proud] the border guards met the invaders with rifle fire and killed several German soldiers, but then their position was quickly overrun, with the loss of one lieutenant of the Orange Regiment...

The broadcast is drowned out by the noise of firing, marching, shouting, and heavy vehicles. We all group together. Day breaks slowly, and the scene lightens. The noise dies down. Father goes to the door and cautiously looks out.

---

2   This was the usual term for a radio receiving set. Here, the two terms may be used interchangeably.

"They've passed. There will be others. Holland cannot defend herself. We can only depend on the French and the British to drive them out."

"What hope is there of that, Father?" asked Gerrit the oldest

"I have no idea. I have never taken an interest in politics and the military. I have always assumed that our neutrality, like the Swiss, would be our defence."

"It seems that the Swiss are safe," volunteered Rudy, "whereas we are not."

"It probably has something to do with our geographical position, and the Swiss banks' willingness to make money out of anyone's accounts."

"You two, Gerrit and Rudy," said Father, "your mother and I will count on for you to do all you can to help and support our youngest, especially the girls, Ina and Ria. We do not know what the future holds for us, or how long this war will last. We must be prepared for the worst. While the Germans occupy our country, we will never collaborate with them. We will have to cooperate, perforce; but collaborate, never! We will be polite, whenever we are forced to deal with them, either on a business footing, or in chance encounters. But we will never be friendly, and never invite them into our home, no matter how much they try to appease us. Let us just hope that life will return to normal as quickly as possible, and that the four of you, Ina, Bert, Ria and Jan, will be able to go back to your studies when, and if, school resumes, as we hope; and that Rudy will continue at his technical school. I will need you, Gerrit, to help me in the garage as usual, and I would not be surprised if the Germans had some sort of maintenance work on their vehicles for us to do. That we can do with a clear conscience."

They had a brief exchange of views; and reached a general agreement of their roles, which concluded with the conviction that if they stuck together as a family all would be well.

* * *

Later that day, they gathered again to listen to this proclamation broadcast by Queen Wilhelmina:

> My People,
>
> After all these months during which our country has scrupulously observed a strict neutrality, and while its only intention was to maintain this attitude firmly and consistently, a surprise attack without the slightest warning was launched on our territory by the German forces last night. This in spite of a solemn guarantee that our neutrality would be respected as long as we maintained it ourselves. I hereby raise a fierce protest against this unexampled violation of good faith and outrage upon all that is proper between civilized states.
>
> I and my government will continue to do our duty. You will do yours, everywhere and in all circumstances, each in the place he occupies, with the utmost vigilance and the inner peace and devotion which a clear conscience affords.[3]

"That's the Germans for you every time," was Mr Mollen's own personal proclamation. "But their attack looks rather different from the last time."

---

3   The text of this speech, as of all others which are quoted in this book, have been transcribed from *Lonely but not Alone* by H.R.H. Wilhelmina Princess of the Netherlands (New York, McGraw-Hill, 1960). The opening phrase, "After all these months," refers to the period from September 1st 1939 when the Germans invaded Poland, to this day, May 12th 1940.

III.

The days pass with dizzying speed, and every day the radio bulletins bring worse and worse news. The Germans, having launched their *Blitzkrieg* against Holland, Belgium and France on May 12th, as we have seen, had made such devastating inroads that both the French and British armies were hurled back with great losses of men and material.

The Royal family and the government of Holland were persuaded to seek refuge in London, where they felt they could do more good than by staying at home, and were evacuated in a British destroyer. The news of their escape spread throughout the country, and was applauded by the people, and by none more warmly than the loyal Mollen family.

So it was that they were eager on the following day to hear the proclamation broadcast by the Queen to her people:

> When it had become absolutely certain (she said) that we and our ministers in the Netherlands could no longer continue to exercise our authority freely, the difficult but inevitable decision had to be taken to transfer the seat of government to a foreign country, for as long a period as will be necessary. The government is now in England. It wishes to avoid a governmental capitulation. Thus all of the Netherlands territory that is still in our hands, in Europe and in the East and

West Indies, continues as one sovereign state to make its voice heard in the community of states.

I make a point of stressing that the civilian authorities in our occupied territory, and any of our people who cannot avoid working for or with the Occupying forces, should continue doing everything that can serve the interest of our own people and in the first place should help to maintain peace and order.

Our heart goes out to our fellow-countrymen at home, who will be forced to live through difficult times. But in the end the Netherlands will recover, with God's help. Remember the disasters and misfortunes that our country has overcome in its history, and do all that you can in the best interests of us all, as we shall surely do our part. Long live the Fatherland!

When the Queen had finished, Mr Mollen switched off the radio, and all were silent for several moments, as they gathered their thoughts, and looked at each other. It was Mr Mollen who broke the ice.

"The Queen seems to know more than she is telling. The war has only just begun, yet she sounds like the voice of gloom and doom."

"At least Willie is safe out in Indonesia," said Mrs Mollen. "I do hope we will hear from him soon."

On the following day, listening to the news for the least glimmer of hopeful news, they learnt of the bombing of Rotterdam by the German air force, a murderous attack carried out without a word of warning. The entire centre of the city was destroyed in an attack lasting a good two hours of terror.

DESTRUCTION OF ROTTERDAM

"To think," Mr Mollen said, "that our authorities were actually negotiating with the Germans at the time and had agreed to a cease-fire. That will be a warning to us all always to bear in mind what evil people we will be dealing with."

IV.

On May 28th, the King of the Belgians surrendered without warning the Allies; the Germans surged forward, drove a wedge between the British and French armies, and forced the British back on the coast of Northern France. They were faced with three daunting decisions: fight on and risk annihilation; surrender; or attempt an evacuation.

It was the Germans who decided the issue for them. Inexplicably—historians have debated the decision ever since—Hitler ordered the German army to halt their northern march, when the British were concentrated in a small area centred on the fishing town of Dunkerque.

During the days of May 27th to June 3rd, over three hundred thousand British and French troops were evacuated safely back to England in an operation which, when successful, was heralded as "the miracle of Dunkirk."

Though many people believed it was a deliverance wrought by divine intervention, which ordained extraordinarily placid seas in the English Channel for three whole days, those who carried it out knew that it was a feat achieved by exceptionally brilliant improvisation.

The officer in charge of this "Operation Dynamo", Admiral Ramsay, appealed to private vessels of every kind and size, around the English coast from Cornwall to The Wash, to sail across to Dunkirk and pick soldiers up from the beaches and ferry them out to the larger vessels waiting off-shore. This operation was carried out in the teeth of constant bombing and *strafing* of the troops on the beaches and the hundreds of vessels scattered over the seas.

The rout of the French forces continued apace, and Paris was occupied. The French Government fled to Vichy. They refused to parley with the Germans, and were replaced by an old soldier of the First World War, Marshal Pétain. This man established a new government, opened negotiations with Germany, and signed an Armistice on June 25. While other countries which were overrun, notably Poland, The Netherlands, Denmark, and Norway, established Governments-in-exile in London, the French became the sole government which collaborated actively with the Germans, and thereby retained their own national government.

With Germany occupying and ruling the whole of Europe from Poland in the east and France in the west; from the Baltic in the north to the Mediterranean in the south, only Britain remained to defy Germany and to carry on the war alone. But what could Britain do? Only her Navy and her Air Force remained intact, and neither was capable of prosecuting the war against Germany. They could only stage an aggressive defence. Would that be enough? How long could they last? Would Germany attempt an invasion?—launch a blockade and siege of the island with fleets of submarines?—bomb their Navy and destroy their cities from the air and force their surrender?

Their strategic position looked hopeless. And helpless, for none of Britain's Dominions and Commonwealth countries could do anything to help. And the United States was divided between those who wished to help and those who insisted on a strict neutrality. Moreover, most American opinion was of the view that Britain was doomed—doomed either to defeat, or to the humiliating necessity of negotiating peace.

Winston Churchill, who had replaced Neville Chamberlain as Prime Minister on May 10, issued this stern warning, and hope, in the House of Commons on June 18. This speech, with its message of warning and hope and defiance, the Mollen family in

Arnhem listened to with renewed feelings both of alarm and of trepidation :

> What General Weygand called the Battle of France is over. I expect that the battle of Britain is about to begin. Upon this battle depends the survival of Christian civilisation. Upon it depends our own British way of life, and the long continuity of our institutions and our Empire. The whole fury and might of the enemy must very soon be turned on us. Hitler knows that he will have to break us in this island or lose the war. If we can stand up to him, all Europe may be free, and the life of the world may move forward into broad, sunlit uplands. But if we fail, then the whole world, including all that we have known and cared for, will sink into the abyss of a new Dark Age made more sinister, and more protracted, by the lights of perverted science.

The majority of opinion in France thought that Britain, at various times their ancient rival and enemy, was done for. And many would rejoice! Not typical of his fellow-Frenchmen in idea, but nevertheless on the same spiritual level, was the opinion written at the time by the French heretical Jesuit evolutionist, Teilhard de Chardin: "(We) are watching the birth, more than the death of a world...the world is bound to belong to its most active elements. Just now, the Germans deserve to win because, however bad or mixed in their spirit, they have more spirit than the rest of the world." He went on to hail the advent of "this young and vibrant new force which embodied the spirit of the modern age", as against "an anachronistic and almost bankrupt Empire led by a garrulous, aging reactionary" like Churchill, who, with Roosevelt, was "grotesquely antiquated."

Seldom has there been a more startling example of the opinions and judgements of an intellectual being corrupted by ideology.

About this time, towards the end of June, the Mollen family, depressed in the defeated and occupied Holland, are once again assembled in the family room, seated round the wireless, and this is the dispiriting news they were destined to listen to:

Yesterday, at 11 a.m., the new French Government of Marshal Pétain signed an armistice with the German Reich, thus putting the seal on the final humiliation of France. We must now come face to face with the stark reality that Germany has conquered and now occupies the whole of Western Europe and that only England lies between us and ultimate salvation. But Hitler is preparing for the invasion and conquest of England; and we know that the British Army, lucky though it was to escape back to England at Dunkirk after its devastating defeat in France, lost all its war *matériel* and can therefore be totally incapable of preventing an invasion of England...

V.

By now the Occupation, military control, and pacification of The Netherlands had been completed. The Germans, knowing as they did the sympathy of the Dutch people for the French and British, and for the Allied cause in general, nevertheless made attempts to seduce Dutch citizens and businesses to their side. And if seduction didn't work, threats and violence sometimes did.

They did not have all the resources needed to sustain their occupation forces while the military campaign was being waged. In particular, they needed food supplies, communications, power, and transport services.

So it was that one day, Mr Mollen received the summons to present himself at the German Army Command established in Arnhem, at 13 Wilhelmstraat. He had no choice in the matter. He would cooperate, perforce; but he would not collaborate. Accordingly, at the appointed hour on the stated date, he lined up to find what they wanted. He presented himself, not in business suit and tie, but in his greasy working overalls.

He was told to wait. In the waiting room he joined a dozen or so other men, who had equally been summoned. A few of them he knew and recognized, and greeted in the customary friendly fashion.

The room was bare: no tables, and no reading materials. But it was dominated by a portrait of Adolf Hitler on the wall facing the door, so that all could see it, and be intimidated by it, as they entered, and sat there, with that face glowering down at them.

One by one the men were called in, and one by one they trooped back out, after varying periods of interview. Some looked depressed and gloomy; others had a sort of smirk on their faces. They were not allowed to stay and talk to those still waiting, but were chased out unceremoniously.

Finally, it was Mr Mollen's turn. As he stood up to go in, the man who had just come out went over to the portrait, stared up at Hitler, and raised his hand as if to make a vulgar gesture. At that very moment the soldier turned round, saw him, and shouted at him. The Dutchman hesitated not a second before converting his gesture into the Nazi salute and cried out:

"*Heil Hitler!*"

The soldier marched over to him and would have clubbed him with his rifle, had Mr Mollen not stepped in between them, stayed the soldier, and said to him sternly:

"What do you think you are doing? He is saluting your Fuhrer."

"He was about to insult him?"

"How? Show me!"

The German soldier was on the point of repeating the Dutch gesture when he realized the trap he was about to walk into. At that moment, the Mollen name was called again. He turned to the soldier and invited him to go in with him and explain. He declined.

Mr Mollen went over to the door, opened it slowly, entered, closed the door behind him, looked around, took in the situation—a table with three officers seated behind it—and sauntered over to face them. There was no chair for him to sit on, so he stood there facing them in expectation.

"You are Herr Mollen?" said the officer in the middle.

"No. I am Mijneer Mollen. We are in the Netherlands, and we speak Dutch."

"You are under German rule, and we speak Germans. Do you understand German? I will speak slowly."

Father nodded. "Yes, provided you understand Dutch if I speak *v-e-r-y* slowly."

"Good! We understand you are an auto mechanic, and a competent one. We have made inquiries."

"You didn't need to. I could have told you. Who did you ask?"

"That does not concern you. You will do maintenance work on our vehicles, as required. We will pay you according to established rates in occupied countries. You have no choice, either to accept or refuse. Do you understand?"

"Yes, I understand. May I have a contract?"

The officer stood up, glared at Mr Mollen, and said, patting the Luger in its holster attached to his belt:

"This is your contract! That is all! Go! Next."

Mr Mollen went back to work, and the relative peace and security of his garage. And the work came to him, a lot of work which kept him and his two oldest sons busy.

VI.

Two weeks later, in mid-July, the Mollens were having their customary breakfast together, and their thoughts and talk turned again to the effects the war was having on them as a family. They agreed that the disturbance of their lives had been rather less so far than they had feared. Even so they lived from day to day, ever fearful of what the next would bring. The event that preoccupied them, inevitably, was the way that the war had been carried against England. England was their, that is Holland's, and Europe's, last and only hope. Would England survive or would she too be defeated and occupied?

The radio—and, amazingly, radios were still permitted—was their sole link with the outside world and the sole source of more truthful and reliable news than the 'information' spewed out by Dr Goebbels, the Nazi minister of information, and his propaganda agencies.

It was thanks to the BBC that the Dutch people became privy to the progress of the Battle of Britain throughout that summer of 1940, and were able to quiz their German captors, discreetly, about their claims of success made by the Luftwaffe—claims advanced often enough to please their masters—without arousing suspicions about their sources of information. As the summer advanced, as July passed and August passed, and September came, with no claims of victory, the good Dutch people as a whole discerned a noticeable decline of confidence and enthusiasm in the German military, and took their signs to presage an impending failure of their aerial assault against England. This good news was reinforced by the news bulletins they all heard from London.

The following two weeks confirmed all their dearest hopes, that the Battle of Britain was a victory for the British air force and Germany's first serious military black-eye. This victory meant, as Mr Mollen had said at the time, that the war would be a long war of attrition which Germany could not win. Everything hinged on when and whether the United States would be drawn into the conflict.

The Germans, for their part, more out of frustration and revenge than any hope of victory, began a campaign of bombing British cities by night with the avowed aim of breaking the spirit of the people and of forcing the Government to sue for peace. It did not happen.

"We have heard enough," Mr Mollen said. "We must have courage. We have nothing to look forward to but years of privation under the German occupation. It is pointless even to talk about rescue and liberation. I have said before that we will be forced to cooperate, but we will not collaborate. We will not make things easy for the enemy, we will never forget that they are the enemy, and we will do everything possible to frustrate their evil purpose. It is a good thing that the Government in its wisdom has stockpiled enough food throughout the country to last us for years. Let us always bear in mind that our hope will be kept alive by our contact with the outside world. We must do everything possible to keep our radio, whatever it costs."

"Let us also pray," added Mrs Mollen. "Tomorrow is Sunday. We know what we have to pray for. I can almost hear the sermon: 'Except the Lord build the house, they labour in vain that build it...

Except the Lord keep the city,
the watchman waketh but in vain.
It is vain for you to rise up early, to sit up late,
To eat the bread of sorrows:

For so he giveth his beloved sleep.
Lo, children are an heritage of the Lord:
— and the fruit of the womb is his reward.
As arrows are in the hand of a fighting man,
So are children of the youth.
Happy is the man that has his quiver full of them...

PART ONE
OCCUPATION
1940 - 1944

I.

Mama was busy in the kitchen preparing lunch. She glances at the clock. My word! Ten-thirty already. She went to the back door and called out to the garage. Papa came in, wiping his hands on a cloth as he went to the sink to wash them.

"Here's your coffee, dear, such as it is. Come and take your weight off your feet for a few minutes. You work so hard"

"'Such as it is'. Yes, it's been quite a time since we had real coffee. Mind you, this is the best quality of rye, and beautifully roasted. I wonder what acorn coffee tastes like? But you're right: somehow it just doesn't taste the same."

He lights his pipe, and as he does so Gerrit joins them, and his mother serves him a mug of coffee.

"What a blessing you are always likely to have steady work, even if it does mean working for the Germans."

"Well," said her son, "at least it's only their transport vehicles Papa and I have to work on, and no war equipment. And we've managed to syphon off a bit of petrol and other supplies from time to time, for 'You Know Who'..."

"And also do work for 'them' and charge it to the Germans," added his father. "But we do take care, my dear."

"I know I keep pleading with you, but I don't dare to think of the consequences ..."

"Yes, and you are right to do so. After all, the children..."

He is interrupted by the sound of heavy vehicles, marching troops, and of shouting outside. Shortly after it subsided there is a ring of the doorbell.

"Ah, that must be the Ganses. We must warn them again of the grave danger they are in."

"I must get back to work on that carburettor."

Mother goes to the door and comes back with Mr and Mrs Gans. The Ganses are our neighbours. It is amusing to report that we and the Ganses have been sharing a newspaper for several years. The newspaper we subscribed to was delivered daily, and we took it in turns each week to alternate the delivery. This exchange was continued without interruption, even during the Occupation. This day was the last day of the Gans's week. As Mr Gans handed the paper to Father he said:

"Those Germans are acting true to form, Willem. You will read it for yourself, but they have now issued a decree that we are to listen only to broadcasts from Germany or the Occupied countries. That means we will only get their slanted news."

"Yes," said his friend, "We heard it on the wireless yesterday. But what can they do? They can't spy on everyone in Holland!"

"No, but they have threatened terrible punishments for anyone they catch listening to what they call enemy broadcasts."

"That may be so. It is to be expected. But the chances of their actually catching anyone listening to them are so remote that it is worth the risk. After all, it seems to me that we are going to have to take certain risks to get reliable information, and we are going to need it simply in order to help us to know how we are to act from day to day. Without information we are blind as bats."

The Ganses are Orthodox Jews, and did not work on their Sabbath. Consequently one of us went to their house and lit their fire for them on Saturday in the cold winter months. In the years leading up to the war, and since Hitler came to power and Germany began his pogrom against the Jews, Father had been warning them of the danger they were in.

The Ganses, for their part, argued that they were perfectly safe in Holland, since Holland had been neutral in 1914, and there was no reason to think that Hitler, despite his conquest or occupation of the Sudetenland, Austria, Czechoslovakia, and Poland, had any desires on the Netherlands. It was an argument difficult to counter, since Father had difficulty in believing otherwise himself.

But since Holland had now been occupied, and powerful France defeated and subjected to the condition of a vassal state, the danger was very real that the Jews would be systematically and methodically rounded up and deported to concentration camps, as had happened already, and was happening, in Germany itself. And if the Germans could do it to their own people—even if they gave a new, and sinister, definition of 'their own people'—they would assuredly not spare foreign Jews.

Horror stories began to trickle through to us via various clandestine and other sources, and were hard to believe. And perhaps unsurprisingly, thousands of people, including Jews, did not believe them. The Ganses were among them. Or they preferred to delude themselves.

When, two weeks later, Mother came back again with the Ganses, there was the customary exchange of friendly greetings, as befitted old neighbours.

"Good morning, Leo"

"Good morning, Willem. Good morning, Mrs Mollen. Here is the newspaper, such as it is. The last one this week. Next week it's your turn again."

"The paper gets poorer and the news gets better all the time—if you believe what you read."

"It's the same with the news on the wireless. Nothing but propaganda."

"It's an interesting question whether the news is better when the enemy are winning or when they are losing."

"The news is the same boasting; it's the tone that is different. There's an edge of desperation when they're lying."

"I agree. No doubt they resort to lies because that's all they dare tell Hitler."

Mrs Gans reacted so sharply to that remark that all turned to look at her.

"The sole mention of that horrible name makes me tremble, Henrika. I'm so frightened I don't know which way to turn any more."

Mother tries to console her friend.

"I'm sorry to have to say this, Leo," said Father calmly but firmly, "but I warned you when war came that you had to leave the country."

"I know only too well you did, my friend," replied Mr Gans. "And I remember to my shame what I said then—that we could trust the Germans, and the reports of the pogroms against the Jews were scare tactics..."

"We haven't heard from our friends the Zondags for several weeks," said Mother. "No letter, no word, their telephone disconnected, no answer at their house... I know we'll never see them again. Who said 'No news is good news' I'd like to know?"

"It is all the more urgent that you still try to get out," Father urged them. "I know it's difficult, but it might still be possible to make your way to Switzerland. I could put you in touch with certain people..."

"It would mean leaving everything we have," countered Mr Gans.

"Stay here and lose everything," countered Father. "Leave and at least you save your lives."

"You make it sound so hard..."

"And so clear and simple."

"We'll have to think about it."

"You'll not have to think about it, Leo. You've had time to think, you have to act, and you have to act at once."

Our parents, almost beside themselves, look at each other. Mother takes Mrs Gans to one side and insists with the greatest firmness.

"You must persuade your husband, Emilie. Why is he so stubborn?—or so blind?"

"I've tried... Heaven knows I've tried. What more can I do?"

"You can tell him you're leaving, with or without him!"

"Oh, I couldn't possibly do that."

There was nothing more our parents could do. They had tried their best. But they were fearful that their premonitions would be borne out by events.

II.

We had established our daily routines–or, to be more precise, we had been allowed to restore our daily routines–as closely as possible to our pre-war customs, so far as our schooling was concerned. Father, with Gerrit's and Rudy's invaluable help and pleasant company and support, were as busy as ever with their work assigned by the German authorities. This work was a blessing, because the amount of other work in their line had been reduced to a trickle, and was limited to essential civilian services, such as medical, emergency vehicles, and the municipal officials authorized by the Occupying Powers

* * *

Ina had just turned 18 and was proving a valuable help-meet to Mother, even if she needed a lot of encouragement. My, but she was the shy one, was Ina! As the expression goes, she wouldn't say 'Boo!' to a goose. But we loved her, and made allowances for her quietness. As children, we were all constantly amazed how different we all were, even with the same parents and the same upbringing and education. It's a good thing in every possible way. Just the thought of everyone being the same, or even similar, was enough in itself to make us appreciate everyone else, and the varied contributions each made to the general welfare. And the very fact of our country being invaded and occupied and governed by a hostile and, to us, a barbaric military regime, soon impressed upon us all how much we depended on each other and how much we knew deep in our bones that we survived as a family, and indeed as a people, or we did not survive at all.

But we're getting ahead of ourselves!

Jan is younger than Ina, and is still at school. Or, to be more precise, he is at a Technical College and will be graduating in two years' time. Then there are the youngest, Bert and Ria, who, at 14 and 12, still go to school But it wasn't quite the same school as it had been. Oh, we had the usual lessons in mathematics, of course; but when it came to subjects such as history and geography, our syllabus was prescribed for us by the *moffen*. We had to learn the German language, and we had to courses in German geography, and German history and were meant to learn what a great nation they were, and what a Great Man Hitler was. Phooey! When it came to exam time we didn't care whether we passed or not. At home we learnt our Dutch history and traditions and customs and laws.

Now, we didn't mind learning the German language, because that meant we could read their great authors like Goethe and Schiller and Heine and Lessing. But such was the Nazi regime that they banned their own greatest writers, because of course they were the voices of reason and humanity. We did not need much prompting to understand that if a political regime outlaws its own very greatest cultural figures, it condemns itself by its own actions. In fact, it even became a perverse delight for us to read them for that very reason!

III.

For the following weeks the plight of the Ganses preyed on our minds. By that we mean, especially of our parents' minds. They tried again, once or twice, to persuade them of their danger, and each time they were met with the stubborn refusal, on the part of Mr Gans especially, to leave and to abandon almost everything they had worked for in their lives. Each time he reduced Mrs Gans to tears; and Father almost to exasperation; until finally they gave up, defeated, and knowing what their fate would be.

"To keep putting off a crucial decision, "as Father summed up the situation to Mother, "is asking the Devil to fan the flames."

"I think rather that he has decided–by not deciding, and by letting events take their course."

"I am sure you are right, my dear," said her husband admiringly, "but I have hated to admit it to myself."

Every family in Holland had its own problems. Many were the same; some were unique according to the family's situation, and according as they had 'connections' or not. And it was never possible, in the situation that existed in the Occupied countries of Europe, either to anticipate a problem or–paradox!–to prepare for the unexpected. Such is the nature of tyrannies: they and their agents act without rhyme or reason, on the spur of the moment, unpredictably and irrationally. And generally violently, to intimidate their victims.

It was then, in June of the following year of 1941, that we heard on the wireless what can only be hailed as news that was both encouraging and discouraging. The encouraging news was the announcement that the Germans had launched a massive assault against the Soviet Union. We were greatly discouraged, on the other hand, by the report that the invasion had already resulted in vast casualties in men and *matériel* on the Soviet side, and advances by the German army deep into Russian territory on every front.

*   *   *

We Mollens did not doubt either the fact of the German invasion of the Soviet Union, or the probability of their early successes. But Russia, as Father knew, was a different kettle of fish from the unprepared and unwilling Western democracies. There was to begin with the sheer vastness of the Russian territory. Then their winters! Would Hitler's army be able to achieve the conquest, and the occupation of Moscow, before their winter set in? So many imponderables! So much to hope for! And to fear. We turned to *Radio Oranje* broadcasting from London for the other side of the story, and the very next day, on June 22nd we listened to Queen Wilhelmina again.

> I want to say a few words to you on the occasion of the change in the picture of the war produced by Hitler's sudden treacherous attack on the Russian people, an attack whose whole purpose is to acquire the food supplies and raw materials that his armies need to continue their fight against justice and freedom.
>
> Today it is Russia, but we know that tomorrow or the day after the mighty bulwarks of our civilization and of the principles that are sacred to us, the British Empire and the United States of America, will face the full impact of Hitler's war

machine. For this reason we shall also fight side by side with the people of Soviet Russia, wherever circumstances may demand it. We shall do this without denying our views of bolshevism, which are based on our principles; for we must never forget that we reject the principles and the practice of bolshevism unreservedly.

Indeed our desire to be and to remain ourselves, with the help of God until the furthest future, may well be stronger than ever before.

At this historic moment in the world war I feel united with all of you in our common awareness of the need to be particularly conscious of this intention.

Since last Sunday the enemy has been fighting on two fronts. Since last Sunday bombs have been raining down on his towns, his harbours and his factories from both east and west. The damage and losses inflicted upon him will shorten the war to our advantage.

My thoughts and prayers are with you at all times in your distressful state. May God be with you and strengthen you for the ordeals that lie ahead.

QUEEN WILHELMINA BROADCASTING
FROM LONDON

When the broadcast had concluded, Father switched off the radio; and, returning to his chair he relighted his pipe, and wondered aloud whether the Queen's assessment of Hitler's aims was correct. He and Gerrit and Rudy mused about other motives and aims–among them conquest for the sheer lust of conquest, the ambition to do what Napoleon had failed to do, and a consuming fear of bolshevism; but all were agreed that Hitler had to be defeated first, and then we would worry about Soviet communism.

"Maybe," Jan chipped in, "it would be a thoroughly good thing, if both Hitler and Stalin fought each other to the death."

"Yes, but what really bothers me," concluded Father, "is how long this war is going to last and how long I will be able to continue to buy my favourite tobacco!"

Gerrit volunteered to scour the country, for, after all, as he pointed out, we have transport and petrol, and we have to do a lot of road-testing of **their** vehicles!"

IV.

Father and Rudy were working on a German vehicle when Mother called out to tell them their coffee was ready. They went into the small office at the top of the garage for a welcome break.

"You and Gerrit are a great help, not only with me, but also with helping Mama to support the children,"

"Ina needs a bit of encouragement, it's true. Bert is settling down well."

"At times I am a bit concerned about Jan. At times he doesn't even appear to be with us."

"I agree; but then he lights up and shows a sudden flashes of wit."

"It never ceases to amaze me how Ria, young as she is, well, to see what spirit she shows and ..."

At that moment Gerrit entered.

"How was it, son?" inquired Father. "The didn't give you too much trouble again or question the hours?"

"No, everything went off well. I think they are beginning to trust us after all. But while I was in their office I heard a voice I thought I recognized coming from an inner office. I tried to peer round but they marched me out. I started to set off for home but waited round the corner. Guess who came out shortly after? It was Piet van Dongen. From what I heard, I am sure he is collaborating with the Nazis."

"I will pass the word around discreetly, and we will keep an eye on him. Well done, son."

It was half an hour later when a small squad of uniformed men marched in to the garage where Father and our brothers were working. The senior man detached himself from the squad and barked :
"One of you is Gerrit Mollen?"
"Yes," replied Gerrit. "I am."
"You are to report to the *Organization Todt* Office on Leopoldstraat in Arnheim tomorrow at six o'clock in the morning. Is that clear?"
"Our city is called Arnhem, not Arnheim."
"We call it Arnheim because that is its German name."
"What am I to report for?"
"That is not your business. You will be there on time or you personally and your family will suffer the consequences?"
Without waiting for a reply, he raised his arm in stiff salute: "*Heil Hitler!*"
And so it was that our oldest brother was taken from us, and sent we knew not where. We will not follow him on his call-up interviews, his assignation to work in Germany, and his journey there. Suffice it to say for the moment that we will see him again.
We were also to hear a lot about and from this hated *Organization Todt,* which was to play a large role in our lives. The very next day, for example, Jan and Bertus were marched off and forced to dig ditches for ten hours.
It was only a few days later, if our memory serves us aright, that Ina was very late getting home. In the early evening. Father is reading the newspaper and sipping a glass of water while Mother keeps glancing at the clock.
"It's been six hours now. Where can she be? What can have happened? Ina is always so punctual. She always tells us she's going to be home for supper if she's going to visit a friend."
"Now, now, my dear! Don't work yourself up. I'm sure she's all right and will turn up soon."
"I do hope you're right..."

"Don't you remember Ria was late once before like this? But she came home. She had been picked up and..."

"I know I mustn't show it in front of the children, but more and more every sound startles me, and every silence makes me listen for a sound..."

The door opens suddenly and Ina comes rushing in.

"Heaven be praised!" exclaimed her mother. "Are you all right, child? Where have you been? What have you been doing?"

"I've been peeling potatoes. I was ..."

"That's it! Of course! That's what it was the last time! Except it wasn't potatoes..."

"Hush! Tell us, child."

"Papa's right. When we all left the theatre, the *moffen* were waiting and herded us like sheep to the Army barracks, all twenty of us. We were there for hours. A mountain of potatoes! Our potatoes, stolen from our farms! I'll never peel another potato in my life! Boy, am I tired! By the way, what time is it?"

As soon as they heard voices, Jan, Bert and Ria came bounding down the stairs to rejoin them.

"Now you're home, Ina, we can have supper. We're famished!"

"Thanks for the homely greeting!"

"Didn't you bring any potatoes home with you?" chided Jan

V.

In the evening of December 7th 1941, a date we will all always remember, we were listening to the late night news as usual, it being a Sunday, before going to bed, when the announcer became excited and announced that Japanese aircraft had attacked the American Fleet in Pearl Harbor, Hawaii, and sunk or otherwise put out of action most of their battleships with great loss of life.

It was the German-controlled Radio Hilversum that we were listening to, so there could be no doubt of its authenticity–except, perhaps, in the estimation of damage done. We could not fail to detect the note of gloating, of triumph even, in the announcer's voice, and were uniformly disgusted at the thought that the announcer was a Dutch collaborator.

We did not know what to think–whether it augured ill for us and the outcome of the war, or well. This quandary persisted for several days, while the Germans continued to make propaganda hay out of the perfidious action.

Our parents' thoughts inevitably turned to our eldest brother, Willi, whom we still hadn't heard from.

Our doubts and qualms were settled just a few days later, when we listened to a part of a long-winded rant by Hitler, who, after having blamed England and the United States for all the woes that had unnecessarily befallen Europe, made a declaration of war against the United States.

To say we were overjoyed is to put it mildly! No news could have made us happier! Now, with the United States entering the war on England's side, their victory was assured, and our ultimate liberation with it. Ah, but how long would it be in coming? Never mind! The fact that the Germans would eventually be defeated was enough to warrant a mild celebration. There was only one fly in the ointment that we could see: Would the United States turn her attention to Japan before entering the European war? Or was she powerful enough to take on both at once? Only time would tell. And the Lord knew how much time we had!

In the following months we learnt that the manpower situation in Germany was becoming critical, with the need for front-line soldiers on the Eastern Front increasing urgently. The Todt Organization went into high gear in their drive to round up hundreds of thousands of young men and women in the Occupied countries to work in the factories and mines and workshops of Germany. Among them was Rudy. He was with us one day, as he had been since the beginning; then he, like Gerrit, was gone, we knew not where. It was not only workers who were rounded up.

VI.

The house is dark. It is four o'clock in the morning. All is quiet. The quiet, and our sleep, are suddenly shattered by a loud banging which is enough to waken the dead–and which might well have been meant to do that. The banging–like the hammering of a heavy object on a door–is then accompanied by an equally loud and hostile shouting. Then there is a scream, a woman's scream.

It is the scream that awakens our parents first, though it came from outside the house. They make their way slowly downstairs, in their night attire, lighting their way with a torch. They go to the window and, putting out the light, pull the curtain apart and look out. Lights outside cast a glow into the kitchen. As the scene unfolds, we all–Bert, Jan, Ina and Ria–come downstairs cautiously to join our parents.

"Oh, my God! The Gestapo[4] are taking the Ganses away!" exclaims Mother "Oh, those evil people! We'll never see them again, I know it! Oh, my God, what can we do?"

Then we heard the shouted orders

"**Heraus! Heraus**! Out! **Schnell**! Hurry it up!"

"Where are you taking us?" cried Mrs Gans. "Why are you doing this to us?"

"What have we done to you to deserve this?" pleaded Mr Gans.

"You're *Juden*, aren't you?–Jews? That's more than enough reason."

"We are still in our night clothes. Please at least let us dress."

---

4 '*Gestapo*' is the acronym of *GeheimeStaatsPolizei*BSecret State Police.

"Don't you dare question us. Get in this truck, and quick about it. We don't have all night to waste."

The Gestapo agent gives Mrs Gans a shove. She trips and falls.

"Don't you touch my wife, you brute!" shouts Mr Gans, overcoming his fear with a supreme effort.

He tries to help his wife to her feet and comfort her. As he is bent over her, a second Gestapo thug prods him viciously in the back with his rifle butt. Mr Gans falls. With a struggle he gets to his feet and helps his wife up.

"Get into the truck, and hurry up!"

The Ganses approach the truck, and look at it.

"Why, it's a cattle truck!"

"Precisely! And very fitting! What did you expect, a limousine? Your days of luxury are over. Your evil Jewish ways have caught up with you!"

Mrs Gans looks into the back of the truck, and she is distraught by what she sees.

"Oh, there's Mrs Rooseveld. The poor thing! The Gestapo have got her too."

"Get in, and hurry it up."

Two Gestapo officers prod Mr and Mrs Gans until they have climbed, albeit with difficulty, into the back of the truck. The truck drives off. The shouting and heavy marching resume. Mother is on the point of tears, which she tries bravely to conceal.

"Oh, don't look, children! You mustn't see what's going on. It's too horrible!"

"There are things that children should not see and hear and know," said Father.

"We have to learn to face these things. We have to be brutally honest with ourselves if we are to survive."

"Up to a point, my son," explained Father. "We also have to have compassion, if we are to survive as a family, as human beings."

"Is there nothing that can be done?" asked Mother plaintively, knowing full well the only answer.

"Nothing now, nothing. Before, yes. Nothing now."
"But why are they being taken away?" asked Ria.
"Because they are Jews," explained Father.
"That's not a reason! I don't understand!"
"Who will ever understand?"

TRANSPORTATION OF JEWS

We all troop sadly back to bed, but there is no further sleep that night. Our minds are too oppressed with a stream of unpleasant thoughts and imaginings.

Later that morning, when we children are at school, our parents are having their morning 'coffee'. While Mother is sewing, repairing and altering, Father is reading the newspaper.

We have not been able to buy new clothes for ages. There is a thriving black market in second-hand clothes, and a brisk trade in exchanges. Some families are lucky, in the limited sense that, if they have numerous children, the youngest benefit from hand-me-downs from the elder ones, whereas the older ones, once they grow out of their own, have few resources left to them. Most honest folk will have nothing to do with the black markets, suspecting, correctly for the most part, that they are either criminals or collaborators.

"Well, dear", sighed Mother, "I don't think I'll be able to re-do this shirt any more."

"Your have done wonders as it is."

"I am still worried by what happened to the Ganses. It was horrible. I do so wish the children hadn't seen it. I'll never get over the fear...and the horror on the faces of those poor people".

"The children are growing up quickly. It is well that they should learn the truth–but at what a cost to others."

"Is there any hope of any good coming out of all this. Those poor Ganses ... our friends and neighbours for eighteen years .... I feel such a weight on my heart."

It was on the next day that a friend dropped in to see them, and to tell them that their neighbours, Jewish friends whom they had known for ten years, had been taken away that very night. It seems there had been a mass round-up of Jewish people throughout the major cities of Amsterdam, Rotterdam, Arnhem, Haarlem, and other cities.

Later that same day, another friend dropped round to tell them in the greatest confidence that the Queen would be broadcasting a message on that subject at twelve noon.

We all came together when Father duly tuned in to *Radio Oranje*, and this is what we heard, in part, of the Queen's talk to her imprisoned people:

> I follow your increasing difficulties and sufferings in all fields; and no less constant is my attention to the insecurity of your daily lives, which become harder to bear every day. The bitter distress of thousand of people in prisons and slave-camps; and all the physical and spiritual ill-treatment inflicted upon you by the hated enemy.

I share whole-heartedly your revulsion at the fate of our Jewish countrymen; and with my whole people I feel this inhuman treatment, this systematic extermination of these fellow-countrymen who have lived for centuries with us in our blessed fatherland, and contributed so immeasurably to the enrichment of our civilization in all spheres of intellectual endeavour.

I raise a fiery protest against the fiendish manhunt which the Nazi hordes, assisted by national traitors, are carrying out all over our country.

We have another reason to remember this day or week, or was it the month? It was when Jan was also picked by the Todt people and deported to Germany. And of course he, like Gerrit and Rudy, had no way of getting in touch with us to let us know where they were or what they were doing. Our prayers for a safe kind of work or destination went with Jan. Rudy, we felt, was better equipped to take care of himself. We had our concerns about Jan: after all, he was only just eighteen.

VII.

All was not gloom or doubt, however, for it was at this time we had the first home visit by Gerrit. And what a delight it was to see him again! And not only see him, but see him looking well and healthy.

"Oh, my son, you don't know what joy you bring to our hearts!"

We all crowded round him and pleaded with him to tell them all about his experiences. The questions poured out thick and fast.

"What are you doing?"

"Where have you been?"

"How have they treated you?"

"How did you get away?"

"Have they sent you home for good?"

Slowly the questions petered out, the moment that Gerrit was waiting for; and when Father proposed that we all sit down and he was sure that Gerrit would tell us everything. Which he did. And this is his story.

"I was transported by truck to Dortmund where I found myself in a large reception camp containing several thousand men, mostly, it seemed, from Holland, Belgium, France and Luxembourg.. The Germans carried out a sort of superficial screening process to find out our skills and past work.

"On the fifth day we were assembled in groups of, say, a few hundred at a time, to discover if any of us had any special skills. They were looking for people who had advanced automotive and related engineering abilities, and could speak German. Although somewhat wary, I stepped forward. Two days later, about twenty of us were assembled in a small room, and, when we were all wondering what was up, a well-dressed civilian gentleman came in–accompanied of course by the usual Gestapo or soldiers.

"Each of us was called out in turn and asked a number of questions by him, in German. They were questions about family background, personal habits, mechanical skills, and automotive experience. And also our knowledge of Germany. Later that day I was called in for another personal interview with him, but this time alone. He told me who he was, and offered me the job as his personal chauffeur. He is the owner of a large company. Of course I accepted. And I have been driving him about this part of Germany ever since."

"What is the name of his company?" Father asked.

"He is Herr Oldenkott of ..."

"Not the Oldenkott of Oldenkott Tobaccos?"

"The very same! How do you know?"

"I used to smoke his tobaccos when I was a young man. I can't remember now why I switched. I believe his name is Dutch originally, and he started his business in Amsterdam. Where is his factory today?"

"At Oberhausen, near Duisburg."

"That's right. The company moved there after the First World War."

"He is no Nazi sympathizer, but he has three sons and they have all had to join up. Strangely they are in different Services. The eldest, Andreas, is a U-Boat captain, the second, Robert, is in the Luftwaffe, and the youngest, Hans, is in the army. That reminds me..."

Reaching into his haversack, he pulled out a large package wrapped in heavy brown paper. Handing it to Mother, he said:

"As you know, sugar is used in the treatment of tobacco. Here is some brown sugar. Be careful not to mention it to a living soul or they will have my head! I didn't exactly steal it; but Herr Oldenkott will deny all knowledge of it if it is discovered."

Then the barrage of questions overwhelmed him again! Especially two, repeated:

"Are you well treated?"

"How did you manage to come home?"

"How often can you get away?"

"Herr Oldenkott tells me nothing until, at the last moment, he tells me where we're going that day. I can only get away with his car at week-ends, when he goes home, but I have to leave it at the border; then I don't have too far to cycle. In that case he will either stay there for the weekend or send for a car to drive him back to Oberhausen."

"I can understand why you have to leave the car there," mused Father.

"I must say you look extremely well and fit," added Mother.

"Yes. The boss treats me very well. He is canny too : deep pockets and short arms! I think it is because I am Dutch that he selected me. He wanted me to come back to see you as soon as possible to allay your fears."

"But we haven't asked you the next most important question! How long can you stay?"

"Only until tomorrow evening."

VIII.

Days followed days, weeks followed weeks, and months followed months. In all the passage of time we followed the fortunes of war as closely as we could, especially the war that affected us the closest, the war on what the Germans called the Eastern Front. In their first great thrust through the Russian homeland they came almost to the gates of Moscow. That is where Napoleon foundered; it is where Hitler's armoured butchers were brought to a halt, by the severity of the Russian winter, which the invading troops were ill-equipped for.

We heard a long time later that at the very beginning of the campaign the simple Russian people welcomed the German soldiers as their liberators, thinking naively that they had come to rescue them from the hated despotic Communist regime. Never was a people so disenchanted! If only Hitler had had an iota of sense, of humanity...Ah, the great ifs of history! So it was that Stalin was prompt to turn Hitler's very strength, his overbearing racial obsession, to his advantage and to rally the whole of the Russian people in what he called the Great Patriotic War. Little wonder that the Allies, now the United States and Great Britain, were quick to align themselves with Stalin and his war effort.

We followed this war with great interest, therefore, since it affected us so keenly; and never so intently as in September of 1942 when, on their second great surge forward that summer, the enemy were halted at Stalingrad. The battle raged for months, with horrendous carnage on both sides. Little by little the defenders of their homeland gained the upper hand. This is what we heard on one occasion from a German broadcast:

> ...everywhere on the Eastern Front the attacks against our heroic soldiers by the Communist Red Army hordes are being thrown back with enormous losses. The *communiqués* from the front line report that whole companies of women soldiers are being thrown into the battle to bolster the flagging strength and morale of the Red Army. The use of women soldiers is a measure of how desperate the enemy has become, and of the weakness of the men. Even if their women prove to be more valiant than the men, we will still hurl them back with appalling losses.
>
> Last night several cities of the German Homeland were bombed indiscriminately by the cowardly terror-raiders of the English air force with the sole intent of destroying our people's houses. It is almost routine these days to say that at least fifty of the criminal bombers were destroyed by our night fighters and flak. On the previous day, the American daylight bombers, trying in vain to reach Augsburg, met with an equally punishing series of well-timed offensive strikes by our heroic fighter pilots.
>
> At sea our U-Boat wolf-packs continue to take an enormous toll of Allied shipping in the North Atlantic. Last month alone, they sank no fewer than three hundred and fifteen merchantmen of various tonnage, as well as forty-two armed naval escorts. Our losses were only nine submarines. Most of the crews of two U-Boats were rescued;

but we feel deeply the loss of those brave men in the other seven boats who were carrying out their proper duties against the aggressors according to the orders of our Glorious *Führer*.

By Christmas it was clear that the invaders were going to be crushed. It was then that Hitler demonstrated still more starkly the true nature of Nazism, and confirmed to the world that he cared as little for his own as for the enemy. He ordered no pullout, no withdrawal, no surrender, when 100,000 German soldiers could have been saved. Fight to the end! They tried, and failed, since they starved or froze to death.

We tell all this because it was after Stalingrad that we in Holland began to feel the effects of that defeat. The Nazis turned even more vicious; and the Nazi viciousness became a general viciousness.

Locally, they were on the alert to find fault or to pick a quarrel with anyone, young and old, male or female, on the slenderest pretext. We know from experience. And it was the most trivial thing. It happened one evening when Mother was in the kitchen preparing the family supper and she was startled by a hubbub outside, an altercation, and voices raised is dispute. One of the voices was that of Ria; the other, that of an angry male. She heard Ria explain with indignation:

"Leave it alone. It's mine, I say. You can't have it!"

"I am commandeering it in the name of the Third Reich! Let go of it or..."

Father listens, then hastening to the back door, which opens on to the back lane, he throws open the door.

"What's going on here? Lieutenant, let go of that bicycle. It belongs to my daughter."

"Correction! It **did** belong to her. Now it is mine. I have commandeered it."

"What is your name, and the designation of your unit?"

"That is no business of yours. I will remind you that you are a conquered country and that we Germans who occupy and rule your country are the masters."

"I think you'll find it is my business. I will find out your unit and report you to your commanding officer."

"Don't you dare threaten me, you stupid Dutchman!"

"I recognize your insignia. I do work for your colonel. He will not be pleased when I report your conduct to him."

"Far from your reporting me, I shall report you, and I shall make sure that you do no more work for the German Army. More than that, I will get you deported to a foreign labour camp."

Mother had witnessed the entire argument. She felt it time to intervene. She asked Father to invite the German officer in. He accepted, and found himself in the kitchen with Ria and her parents. Mother made a point of sitting down, and then addressed the officer:

"Excuse me," she said, in fluent German, "but I see no reason to get nasty. Tell me, Officer, you come from Berlin, don't you?"

"Why, yes, I do. But how do you know?"

"It is your accent. You are an educated man. You probably went to the *Gymnasium*, and the *Hochschule*."

"Why, as a matter of fact..."

"Berlin has been heavily bombed. Is your family safe?"

"My mother was killed in a raid last month by those damned English *Terrorflieger*."

"I am sorry. We in The Netherlands have had many hundreds of mothers killed by your friends. It is as if your Nazi friends killed your mother. You have sowed the wind and you shall reap the whirlwind."

The German was taken aback by this accusation, all the more since he was not accustomed to being lectured by a beaten enemy. He opened his mouth to reply, but Mother did not leave him the chance.

"I am really surprised that the Third Reich with its industrial and military might would need to steal a young girl's bicycle. Don't you think that's a bit heavy-handed?"

"Well, perhaps, when you put it like that..."

"How else would you have me put it, Lieutenant? Besides, I thought you German officers were gentlemen?"

"*Ja, ja, gnadige Frau*! Perhaps I was a bit hasty...." Then, turning to Ria, he said:

"You may have your bicycle."

"Thank you, Lieutenant. Before you leave, may I ask you whether you know this poem? —

Du musst herrschen und gewinnen,
Oder dienen und verlieren,
Leiden oder triumpheren
Amboss oder Hammer sein.[5]

"I think I read it at school. It is probably Goethe."

"Yes, it is Goethe. What do you think of it now?"

"He is right! We only conquer and rule!"

"No! You have lost the war. Look at Stalingrad...."

The officer turned red, and almost shouted:

"That is only poetry! It has nothing to do with this war! The first duty of a soldier is to obey orders!"

"Like orders to kill children? ...."

"A soldier does not question the reasons for his orders!"

He marched back to the door, stopped, turned, and, shooting out his right arm stiffly, cried: "Heil Hitler!" and stormed out.

The officer gone, we all sighed a sigh of relief, in the knowledge that the scene was about to turn very nasty. Father turned to Mother, his eyes alight with admiration, and said softly:

---

5 You must either conquer and rule or lose and serve, suffer or triumph, and be anvil or hammer.

"You handled him with great *finesse* and courage, my dear. To think that almost the whole German people have come to think like him."

"Have they, you think? Surely there will be people who hate him like us?"

"If so, they have little chance of doing anything about it."

VIII.

As happens so often in life, some clouds have a slightly silvered lining, storms are followed by a ray or two of sunshine, and sad events are compensated for by happy ones–if we may be permitted to extend the parameters of happiness.

The event which brought a relative, if brief, happiness to us as a family was a surprise visit. We were confronted by no less a person than Rudy, who was making his first return to see us since his deportation to Germany. As a matter of fact, he announced his visit: we heard a loud klaxon outside the house and went to explore. It was Rudy at the wheel of a German truck!

We immediately surrounded him, and besieged him with questions from all angles. When calm was restored, and we all were seated in the family room, Rudy was able to tell us of the events in which he had been caught up. But first, looking about him, he asked:

"Where's Jan?"

"He's gone too. He was picked up by the *Todt* a couple of months ago and of course we haven't heard from him."

"And Gerrit?"

"Yes, Gerrit has been home. We will tell you his story after yours."

"Good. Well, when I left Arnhem I was packed off to Münster. The next day I was trucked out to Dortmund. You probably know that the British have been bombing the industrial cities of the Rühr for months on end, in fact for well over a year, and have inflicted considerable damage and casualties. I was assigned to a large group of men who were being sorted out for work in the bombed towns. I was selected for the job of driving a truck and I am ordered to any city which has been bombed and be loaded with any supplies and equipment that can be salvaged from among the ruined factories and hospitals and warehouses and taking them wherever they are needed...."

"Are you on your own, Rudy?" put in Ria. "Do they trust you with all that stuff?"

"Of course not, silly! I am accompanied—or rather guarded—all the time by a soldier, who has orders to shoot me if I try any funny stuff."

"Where do you live when you're not driving?" asked Ina.

"I am based at Gladbach, a pleasant little town in the heart of the Ruhr, but without any industry. I figure that they house us there so that we won't be bombed and can reach any of the bombed cities as soon as they have cleared the streets."

"How bad is the damaged, son?" asked Father. "Have you been caught in any bombing yourself?"

"The damage is pretty bad; and it is getting worse almost by the day. I haven't been bombed myself. The British only bomb at night, and we go in and salvage what food and other supplies we can during the day. Unfortunately the Americans are bombing German factories during the day, which makes our job riskier. On the other hand we generally get plenty of warning of an air-raid."

"Who does all the work of removing the bomb damage so you can get to the places you have to go to?" asked Mother

"They are men and women from the Occupied countries. I think they are mostly from Eastern Europe. I haven't had the chance to speak to them often. The guards are always on the watch, and won't allow any fraternization. We go into a hospital or warehouse or factory and salvage what we can, and we are always guarded."

"But where do you live when you are not working?" This was Ria's question.

"I live in a large house with about twenty other drivers. It is pretty spartan, I can tell you! But we have enough food. Though no freedom. We are guarded all the time."

"Yet you are allowed to come and see us–and with their truck at that?"

"Yes. I know it seems strange; but the fact is that I think I have earned their trust. I speak their language and they know I'm an expert mechanic. Besides, I know well enough that if I did anything foolish they would take it out on my family. Even so, I think I may have the chance to snitch some food one day. If so, I will find a way to smuggle it in."

"What do you mean by 'smuggle it in', my son?" added Father.

"I am searched at the border, both coming and going. I am going to try to cultivate the border guards, if I can get away more often in future. And if the same guards are there for any length of time."

"Are they German guards, Rudy," asked Bert, "or men from occupied countries?"

"They are all Germans. But they are not all brutes. They are older men, too old for the front line."

"Dear Rudy, you must never take any chances on our account. It just isn't worth the candle."

"Tell me, son: What is their morale like? How are they coping with the bombing, if they are getting it day and night?"

"So far I haven't noticed any signs of cracking. I must tell you something that happened to me a few months ago. I was driving along a long road one night on the way back to Gladbach when it was very dark—and we only have the dimmest driving lights—when I hit something. I was going to stop and find out, but my guard told me to keep going. I refused. I stopped, and went back, and found a German Army motor-cyclist lying in the road. We got him into the truck and drove to the nearest hospital. A couple of weeks later my route took me back to that town, so I visited him and found him recovering...."

"You did a very nice thing, Rudy," said Ina, "considering he was an enemy."

"Maybe; but you just can't run someone over and leave him, it doesn't matter who he is." (Everyone nodded in agreement.) "Unfortunately," Rudy went on, "the story has an unhappy sequel. A week or so later I found myself once again in the same town, and—you know what?—the town had been bombed by the British and the hospital was destroyed."

"And you mean to say, Rudy," asked Mother, "that the man you saved..."

"Yes, he was killed, with hundreds of others."

IX.

Near the end of April 1943, when we were still basking in the relative glow brought on by the German defeat at Stalingrad and the subsequent advances by the Red Army, the whole of Holland was cast into turmoil by the German edict that ordered the call-up of the three hundred thousand Dutch soldiers who had been released after the war. They were to be deported to Germany for work in the factories, mines and ports—and indeed wherever the war machine required them.

Fortunately this edict did not affect us as a family, first because of course Gerrit and Rudy and Jan were already working in Germany; and second because they had not been soldiers, having been exempted by the fact that our family already had one son in the Army, that was Willie.

But it did affect others—and how badly we were soon to learn.

On the late afternoon of the 29th Father received a visit from a friend who worked in the city hall—under strict German supervision. The two men were closeted in the garage for a good half-hour. That evening, after supper, we were all called to the family room by our parents for a talk. By saying "we all", we mean all of us still left at home, which meant only Ina, Bert and Ria.

Our parents looked unusually concerned; and they were not long in confiding in us the cause of their worry. Father told us that there had been a spontaneous strike by the workers at all the various factories which produced war goods at Hengelo in protest against the Nazi edict.

It is no exaggeration to say that on hearing this we children became not a little alarmed.

"Why," said Bert, "Hengelo is only about forty kilometers from here. I think we all know the town quite well."

"That is so," said Father. "We have no idea what the consequences or repercussions will be. But we know the *moffen* for what they are. And we are sure that whatever they do will not be nice. Your Mother and I want you to be most particularly careful about what you do and say during the coming days. Do not say or do anything to anyone that could possibly provoke a reaction. It is a sad thing to say, but we really do not know who could let slip an indiscreet word which would reach the ears of the enemy."

During the day that followed we dared not even listen to our wireless. Yet we managed to get the news. And it was both cheering and frightening.

STRIKERS AT HENGELO

The Barn

The strikes spread to most of Holland. At Eindhoven, the huge Phillips factory was shut down by the workers. In Limburg, in the south of Holland, over ten thousand miners walked off the job. Throughout the countryside, the farmers stopped delivering milk to the dairy plants.

It could not last. And it didn't. After all, the Germans held the upper hand. And they showed it. They took savage reprisals, shooting and arresting workers by the score. We learnt later that there were close to two hundred strikers killed and over four hundred other casualties.

It was all over in no time. Everyone went back to work by May the 5th. But the very nature of the strikes taught both the Germans and us a lesson. For the Germans, the uprising came as a warning that their policy of trying to win over the Dutch people to the German way of looking at the war had failed.

The next thing they did was to confiscate all wireless sets capable of receiving foreign broadcasts. At first the local authorities demanded that the citizens hand in their sets by placing them on the street by the front door. The following week the Gestapo and the troops swarmed throughout every neighbourhood, invading houses and searching every nook and cranny for hidden radios. The luckless people who had not concealed their sets well enough were arrested and despatched to Germany, either for forced labour in their mines and factories or to concentration camps, where they were unlikely to survive.

For us Dutch people, the very spontaneity of the actions came as a heartening sign that we were not crushed or even intimidated by the Nazi reign of terror. Thousands of able-bodied young Dutchmen went into hiding. The Resistance movement won many new recruits. And a renewed energy and initiative was put into the twofold task of disseminating reliable information and stimulating hope among the people and opposition to the hated enemy by means of clandestine leaflets which were printed and circulated throughout Holland.

None of us children at home were involved in these patriotic measures. Indeed, at the time we knew nothing about them. Later, of course, we suspected that Father had a hand in them—at the very least in distributing some of the leaflets, but we were never able to draw anything from him. Mother told us that, much as he was keen to get involved, she forbade him to: his first duty was to protect his family. After all, the man was in his sixties. War was a young man's business.

X.

We were all sitting around doing our various things after supper early one evening when we heard a frightening and unaccustomed noise. We looked at each other nervously, and especially at Father; but he looked as puzzled as the rest of us.

The noise came from above, in the air, and resembled the roaring, almost a screaming, of an engine running out of control. Almost as one, we got up and went outside. Locating the direction of the noise, we searched the sky; and suddenly Bert exclaimed:

"There it is! Look! It's a plane on fire!"

We looked in the direction indicated by Bert and we all saw it at once. It was a huge plane with four engines, except that three of its engines were stopped—we could see the propellers clearly—and flames were coming from two of them. The plane was quite low, and was circling slowly round the town. Suddenly an object fell from the plane, and almost immediately a parachute opened. We didn't know which to watch, the parachute or the plane. We looked form one to the other and back again. Then we concentrated on the plane, to see whether there would be more airmen leave the plane.

The plane came lower and lower, and it seemed as though it must crash on the city. As we watched, both afraid and transfixed, the plane lurched, turned, and seemed to make one last effort to make for open country. Finally it went out of sight, and we heard an awful noise as the plane crashed into the ground; and a cloud of heavy black smoke rose into the air We hoped and prayed that it had missed the houses.

In fact, it had. It transpired that the pilot made a herculean effort to avoid the built-up areas, and had only succeeded in doing so at the deliberate cost of his and his fellow-crewmen's lives. We mourned their loss, amid our sorrow that only one airman had managed to leave the plane in time.

The plight of the plane and of its crew had been followed keenly by several members of our Resistance organization who lived or worked much closer to the stricken plane, and were the first to reach the airman who had parachuted safely to the ground. They helped him to gather up his parachute, and rushed him away from the scene to a safe hiding-place. The only additional information we were able to gather subsequently was that the Germans did not find him, and equally failed to identify the men who had smuggled the American to safety. At other times, the Gestapo would have taken hostages from among the Dutch civilian population and shot them if they had not surrendered the Resistance workers. That they did not on this occasion can only be ascribed to their preoccupation with more pressing matters.

There is a sequel to this drama that has both pleasant and unhappy aspects.

The son of a cousin of Father's was one of the first Resistance men to reach the scene. They cut up the parachute and shared it among them. Later he brought a nice panel of the material and gave it to Ria to make something with. It was the first time that Ria had handled and worked with pure silk. It was gorgeous material, and she made a doll's dress, which she embroidered at the bodice and sleeves in a Swiss dirndl style. Everyone thought it was extremely pretty; and Ria was very proud of it. After the war it was passed round among nieces and cousins, and got 'mislaid'. Ria never saw it again.

XI.

"Look, it's five o'clock...."

"The children should be home soon."

"Children! We have only two left at home...and how they have grown up in four years!"

"You're forgetting me!" exclaimed Ina.

"Not forgetting, Ina, far from it. You are a young woman, and... That reminds me, Ina— will you go and my pipe, please? I left it in the garage somewhere...you'll find it."

With Ina gone, Father goes over to the bookcase, removes a panel of empty books bound together, and reveals the radio. We all learnt later that our parents had kept the radio a secret from us so that we would not be tempted to blab to friends in an unguarded moment some information that could not have come from a German source. After about thirty seconds a voice is heard :

> This is the BBC European Service broadcasting to France, The Netherlands, and Belgium. Here is the latest news bulletin. The Second Front invasion of the Continent was launched three days ago and the Allies have established a solid beachhead at five points on the Normandy coast. At three of the landing sites, columns of infantry supported by artillery and armoured forces are penetrating inland. Round-the-clock bombings of rail and road communications are

preventing enemy reinforcements from reaching critical areas. Now that the landings are secured and ensured by a total mastery of the air by our fighter forces, we will be broadcasting an updated communiqué every hour. On the Eastern Front the Russian offensive continues to gain ground at every point and German resistance...

Our parents looked at each other with an expression announcing a joyful optimism on hearing this news when Mother suddenly looks about her and gets up.

"Someone is coming!"

Father hurriedly returns the wireless to its hiding place. The door opens and Ria enters hurriedly and closes the door behind her.

"You're all out of breath, child. Why have you been running so hard?"

"I kicked a German officer!"

"Kicked a German officer? How on earth...?"

"He hit me first! I was walking back home from school with Hettie .... come to think of it, it's the first time I've ever walked home with her. I didn't even know she lived in this direction. Anyway, we were walking down Willemstraat—and you know how narrow the pavement is—and along come these two S.S. officers towards us. When they got close, Hettie and I stepped into the road to let them pass. And when they drew level—I was nearer to them—one of them slapped me in the face and shouted at me: 'That will teach you not to insult a German officer!' I don't know what got into me, but I was so mad that without thinking I gave him a great kick in the shin, and I took off like the wind. I know the back streets and alleys better than they do, and as you know I can run, so I soon lost the damned *moffen* ..."

"Think no more of it, my dear," said Father. "We'll look after them, if the need arises. You did well to run ..."

"Your father is right. But just watch your language. What worries me is what became of Hettie?"

"I don't know. She didn't keep up with me, or she took a different route".

"You can't go out again, but you will have to see to it tomorrow at school that she's all right."

It was at this point that Ina returned to say she couldn't find Father's pipe. And Bert walked in a few moments later.

With the family assembled, Father told them about the radio and cautioned them to secrecy. He then announced the wonderful news about the launching of the Second Front by the Allies, with the invasion of Normandy three days ago.

Ria jumps up and dances in an ecstasy of joy. And just as abruptly she stops.

"But Normandy is so far away! They'll never be here!"

"Of course they will, silly! I wouldn't have told you if I'd thought..."

"That's right," put in Mother." But now you'd all better get ready for supper."

Before we can leave, the door bursts open and a German soldier enters. He is older than most soldiers. Our parents told us later that we looked very apprehensive, while trying not to, and glancing questioningly at each other. The German soldier tries to appear authoritative, but he is not convincing. Father goes over and faces him:

"What's this all about, soldier? What d'you think you're doing....?"

"Well, who did it?" he shouted. "Who's responsible?"

"Who did what, soldier? What are you talking about?"

"You know what I'm talking about. I saw her come in!"

"Saw who?"

"A girl. Is she your daughter?"

"I have a daughter. I have several daughters.[6] What is she supposed to have done?"

"That's the one! Over there! I saw her!" Then: "Done? Done, you ask! It's the light, *Dummkopf!*"

"What light are you talking about, soldier?"

"The light on the roof! There was a light shining on the roof!"

"A light on the roof? What light are you talking about?"

"I saw it myself. Were you trying to signal to enemy aircraft?"

"It was probably the reflection from a window. You call me *Dummkopf*. You are the *Dummkopf*, to think that I would signal to Allied aircraft so they can drop their bombs on us, their friends."

"We're ready for anything since the enemy landings..."

"Ah, yes, the Allied landings in Normandy. How are they going—for you, I mean?"

"We are hurling the enemy—your friends and Allies—back into the sea, just as we did at Dunkirk in 1940!"

"Then how do you explain that the Allies have already penetrated as much as thirty miles inland?"

"How do you know that?"

"Ah, that's what the light was! It was a signal to a pigeon, which has just alighted here. It had a message attached to its leg. The message read: "Dear Mr Mollen, The Allies have landed and will be in Paris in June, in Arnhem in July, and in Berlin before Christmas. Your friend, Winston Churchill.""

The four of us couldn't help it, it must have been the relief, but we suddenly burst out laughing. The soldier was utterly discountenanced, and according to character resorted to threats.

"I will report you to the..."

"To whom? Soldier, let me give you a word of advice..."

---

6   This was true. The eldest daughter, Ennie, was married and lived in Rotterdam.

The Barn

Suddenly an S.S. officer strides in, threateningly, through the still open door. Father wastes no time in sizing up the situation, and continues, on a different note, to the soldier:

"Yes, Corporal, you are quite right. I am so sorry. I will discipline my son. I keep telling him..."

The S.S. officer looks suspiciously around the room; then goes over to the soldier.

"Is everything in order, soldier?"

Ja, ja, Herr Kapitein! Everything is in order."

XII.

The whole family are gathered round together and discussing the latest startling, and encouraging, news.

"Papa," exclaimed Ria in excitement, "do you really think the Allies will be here in a month or two?"

"Yes, I do. Once their Armies break out from their bridgeheads and build up their heavy armour—why I'll wager they'll liberate Paris by August and be here before winter. Ria, go and get the map—you know where it is."

Ria runs off. She is back in a few moments with a map, which she opens out on the table, and we all crowd around. Father puts his finger on it and explains:

"They will have to capture a large port. Look, here's Le Havre. But then, beyond there, to liberate Belgium and us they'll need to capture Antwerp intact, before the Krauts—I like that American term: the Krauts!—can blow it up. If they can do that we'll possibly be liberated by Christmas."

"Oh, Papa," Ria exclaimed with passion. "If only…I'm so sick of this war and these Germans, and… and…!"

"And everything," added Ina.

"We know how you feel, my dear," Mother sympathized. "We're all sick of them. But, as your Father says, it can't be long now."

'Why don't we hang the map on the wall?" suggested Bert. "Then we can all watch the progress of the Allies."

"A great idea!"

We all take a hand in hanging the map; and then silently measure the distances between the Allies' positions, Le Havre, Paris and Antwerp, and their location.

"We had better conceal it," Father says. "Do you have anything we can hang over it?"

Mother leaves the room saying that she will find something. When she returns with something that looks like a tapestry, Father nodding approval, says:

"Now, what if we have a little celebration? I have a bottle of *Genever* tucked away, and I wouldn't be surprised if Mama didn't have something..."

He fetches a tray of small glasses and a bottle. He pours a little for each, except Ina, Ria, and himself. Then, turning to Mother, he asks:

"Do you think the girls could have a sip, my dear?"

"I don't think it will do them any harm, for once."

"Hey, they're finally treating us like grown-ups!"

"But what about you, Papa?" inquires Ina

"Yes, where's your glass?" chimes in Ria.

"Yes, surely you can break down on an occasion like this, Papa?"

"What occasion? What are you talking about?"

"Don't you remember? Father swore off liquor before we were born."

"Then how would I remember, silly!"

"I remember something vaguely. There must be a story behind it."

"There's a story behind everything, if you look," added Father enigmatically.

"There's no story behind me, I hope!" chirped Ria.

"There's a story behind your name, Petronella! Isn't there, Dad?"

"I don't want to hear it again, ever, I hate it!"

"What about your not drinking, Dad?" inquired Ina

"Ah, that's another story...eh, Mother?"

"That will be for another time."

"Do tell us! What's the ghastly secret?"

The parents ignored the question; and Father changed the subject.

"A toast! Here's to the end of the war!"

They all took a little sip. Ina and Ria sip, then gag, and finally spit out their drink, while their brothers laugh.

"Ugh!" they splutter in unison. "It tastes like lavatory disinfectant."

"How do you know?" teased Bert.

*   *   *

At that instant their moment of merriment was shattered and their celebration cut short by a loud hammering on their front door— the noise which this family, like everyone in the Netherlands, as indeed in all the Nazi-occupied countries, were accustomed to and had come to dread. Father did not hesitate before indicating to us to cover the map, and beckoning the boys to accompany him.

They had hardly reached the front room than they were met by the vulgar invasion of four jack-booted soldiers. One of them advanced, to be confronted by Mr Mollen.

"What do you want?"

"Papers! All of you. **Schnell!**"

We all fetched our papers, except Ria. The Germans examined them suspiciously, and returned them slowly, with seeming reluctance. Then, to Ria:

"Where is your ID card?"

Father answered for Ria: "My daughter is not yet of age."

"How old is she?"

"Fifteen."

"She is to go to the Commissariat tomorrow to be photographed."

RIA'S ID CARD

The man in charge then demanded to know whether he, Mr Mollen, knew, or had seen, Herman Wiersma. He was able to persuade him that the person was completely unknown to him.

"If you meet him you are to hold him and take him to the Commissariat."

The Germans were on the point of leaving when none other than Gerrit entered the open door and appeared before them.

"Gerrit!" we all shouted in one voice. But it was Mother who reached him first and threw her arms about him.

"Who are you?" demanded the German officer.

Gerrit advanced, stated his name, and produced his papers.

The German took his time examining them before handing them back.

"How did you get here from the German border point?"

"By bicycle. It is outside. Come, I will show you."

Gerrit led the Germans out. After a few moments he returned alone.

XIII.

Those days following the Allied landings in Normandy were the most exciting of our lives. We followed the Allies' rapid progress through France and Belgium after their successful break-out from Normandy.

Like the many people we knew locally, we had an increasing, and increasingly optimistic, interest in the Allied military advances. Yet our optimism was severely tempered. By early September the Allies had only got as far as Montreuil. There their offensive seemed to stall. They seemed to be concentrating their efforts on the liberation of France, rather than on winning the war. That was Father's view of the situation. His view was that the Allies' strategic thrust was dictated by political interests, not military. What had the French done to further the war effort? On the contrary, they had collaborated with the Nazis. Could the Allied military people not see that the way to Germany, and to Berlin, lay through Belgium and Holland, not via Paris? War should be conducted by soldiers, not by politicians! What do politicians know of strategy and tactics? We were all poring over the map yet again one evening, talking about the situation, and wondering what the Allies would do next and how long it would take them to liberate us, with our minds concentrating on their conjectures and hopes and doubts, when, not having heard the door open and close, we all suddenly heard an unaccustomed noise, looked up, and there saw Jan. We all gasped as if we had seen a ghost.

"Hey, what's the matter? Don't you remember me?"

"Yes, but ..."

Father was the first to recover his wits.

"My dear boy, welcome home!"

Mother rushed to embrace him; and, taking him by the arm, led him to an easy chair.

"You look so tired! Take your time and then tell us what has happened. In the meantime I will get you something to drink."

"I could do with a bit more than .... I'm famished."

"Of course, how thoughtless of me. I'll go and get you a meal right away."

Mother hurried out to the kitchen and returned within the quarter-hour with a plate of food.

"Your favourite, dear–an *uitsmijten*.[7] And a glass of beer. But the meat is not ham, and I'm afraid you will have to imagine the eggs."

Jan tucked in pretending it was the real thing, basking in the admiring, and wondering, looks of all gathered around him. When he had finished, and was savouring the last of the beer, he stretched, gave a huge yawn, and looking round him at his family with a look that can only be described as relief and affection, said:

"I've been walking for hours and I'm dog tired. I'm afraid I'm going to have to go to bed now. I'll tell you all about it tomorrow."

Of course we had no choice. Jan looked dead beat and we all wished him a Good Night! as he made his way upstairs to his bedroom.

Jan slept for twelve hours. When he came down to breakfast the next morning he looked refreshed and rested, Even so he took his time before rejoining us in the family room, where we all waited expectantly for his news. Finally we were all assembled and Jan began his story.

"You remember when I had to report to the Commissariat at six o'clock that morning. There were a lot of us, all pretty young

---

7   Two slices of buttered bread and ham topped with fried eggs.

like me. We were taken by lorry to the railway station and all herded on a train. It left immediately but we had no idea where we were headed, except we knew it was somewhere in Germany. We travelled for a good three days. We were only let out once a day, one wagon at a time; and were given only the barest rations of bread and sausage. When we finally arrived and were ordered out it was dark, but I caught a glimpse of the station name. It was Wolgast. Someone said we were on the Baltic coast. From there we were marched all night and half the next day. We finally arrived at an encampment surrounded by barbed wire and look-out towers with armed guards. There was no sign of any kind. We were marched into the camp and told to dump our gear on the ground between two buildings. We were then marched into a small inner compound and given tools of all kinds—picks, shovels, buckets, crowbars, you name it. We were then marched farther into the camp and saw what we were there for: the place was a ruin and there was a mass of wrecked buildings. Our job was to clean up the rubble so they could start rebuilding.

"Rumour had it that the damage had been caused by explosions, but we all knew from our experience that it had been caused by Allied bombing. We wondered what there was there so important to attract the bombers. Little by little we heard the facts. It was Peenemunde, and the Germans were carrying out secret tests on long-range rockets. Agents got wind of it and got the word out to British Intelligence. The devastation was huge and hundreds of people were killed. As it happens, one of the housing areas full of Polish workers a couple of kilometers from the main site was hit by mistake and that is why they rushed us there. We had been there about three months when a chap I had palled up with and I decided we'd had enough. One night when it was overcast and the air raid siren went off we managed to slip out during the confusion.

"We walked all night to get as far from Peenemunde as possible, and the next day made our way back to Wolgast where we took a train going west after several hours' wait. We had our passes, of course, and some money, and we were not challenged at first. Hans and I decided we had to stick together if we wanted to survive and get back home in one piece.

"We took a train only about fifty kilometers from Wolgast. We had to conserve our money. I remembered lessons at school, and also what you taught us about making do with what you have. What little we had we needed for food. It's a good thing Hans and I agreed. So we walked. We walked for days; we walked for two or three weeks. We kept to the small roads and avoided the large towns. But in that part of the world there are no large towns; and the going is fairly easy. The countryside is fertile and pastoral, and we found vegetables to eat, even raw, to eke out our dwindling funds.

"But we were concerned with winter coming on and knew we could not keep walking. So we decided to look for work with a farmer. We figured that even Germans poisoned by the Nazi racial virus might look favourably on Westerners. As it happens, all the young people had been called up for war service and the farmers were short handed. I guess we were lucky. We found a farmer who was desperate for help and when we showed our passes and explained our situation truthfully, he took us on. We learnt we were in the district of Wendland. I don't think I ever heard the name of the nearest town. He is a dairy farmer, and he was busy all winter. They had two sons away at the war, called up despite their pacifism, which of course they dared not declare. And a sprightly young daughter of about twelve..We lived with the family and they treated us very well. It turned out they were Lutherans, which may have something to do with it. We could gladly have waited out the end of the war there, but you know the old saw: All good things must come to an end. Spring was in the air; home was calling again; and with the farmer's blessing we left. They were lovely people and I will not forget them. We left, Hans and I, early one morning, with haversacks containing toilet things and a change of clothes, and walked for several hours to the nearest railway station. The farmer paid us well and even gave us a bonus for our travels. Hans and I decided to take main line trains and even to risk the major cities this time, for the shortest route to Holland.

"Our immediate destination was Hanover, which we figured was about a hundred kilometers away. By now, of course, our German was pretty good; and even though we had foreign identification, we had no difficulty in finding beds in a hostel near the station, late at night though it was. The next day we went straight to the railway station to find out about trains going west—and especially to see whether they still ran to Holland. Would you believe they did! Most of them were troop trains, but civilian officials also had business in other countries such as France and Belgium and Holland, and rail was their only way of travel. But what amazed us was the damage in the heart of the city. The destruction of buildings and whole streets was staggering. We had never seen or imagined anything like it. The British were certainly giving back to the Germans all and more than they had done to Warsaw and Rotterdam and London. Our luck ran out, and we could not escape the dragnet put out by the Todt Organization. We were put to work that very day and for next several weeks with shovels and barrows in clearing up the bomb damage. At night we were kept under close guard in a compound outside the city, until, one day, we got even worse news. We were going to be shipped east to other cities that were even worse off. Hans and I began to regret leaving our farm. At about midnight we were all assembled and marched under guard through the town to the railway station. By this time I had learned that when you're on the lam to look out for traps, and when you're in the box to keep an eye out for a way out. We were marching through the town when suddenly the air raid sirens started their howling and all the street lights went out and the traffic disappeared. Our guards brought out torches and shouted at us to keep close together. I spotted a narrow side street, tapped Hans on the arm, and scooted up it and hid in a doorway. Hans didn't follow me. I never saw him again. I waited perhaps five minutes, quaking like a jelly, until all was quiet, then crept out and started walking as quickly as possible in the opposite direction hugging the buildings. I heard the droning of engines in the sky, and about a dozen thin pencils of light searched the sky for the bombers. There was just enough starlight to see by and in less than an hour I found myself in open country. I decided the best thing was to walk at night and to lie low during the day. I could drag this story out but you'll be glad to hear it's almost over. I had an amazing piece of luck. I found a bicycle. The owner must have been a tall man because the saddle was far too high. I managed to ride out for about a mile before checking for tools. It had a saddle-bag, with tools. And a spanner. And, lo, the saddle came down. I decided to ride during the day now like an honest man and I rode like the wind and found cheap inns in villages at night and was never challenged. I finally made it to Emmerich where I had to leave the bicycle and sneak across the border at night. And here I am!"

We all exclaimed our admiration for Jan's daring exploits and escapes, and particularly bemoaned the loss of his friend Hans. We besieged him with questions, and particularly wondered whether he had left out any exciting details. Ria was interested to know more about the farmer's daughter and whether she was pretty! And Jan hadn't told them the farmer's name. No, he had asked Jan particularly not to. His account of the bomb damage in Hanover confirmed the reports brought home by Gerrit and Rudy; and Jan thought that the Germans' morale, though shaken, was not yet cracking. But the attitude of the city people was different from that of the country folk, who were not going through the same experiences. Jan added that he tried to paint a gloomy picture of events for the Germans wherever he stayed overnight.

The next day was Sunday, September 17th. When we—all except Jan, who was still resting up—arrived back from church, we youngsters exuded what our parents called later "a palpable air of dissatisfaction". And we weren't slow in voicing it.

"The Church has run out of wafers but not out of sermons," moaned Ria.

"My child, one does not go to Mass only for Communion," admonished her mother.

"I'm with Ria," said Bert. "What does one go to Mass for? What are all the prayers and sermons doing for us? We have been praying for help and hope for four years and where has it got us?"

"I think," Father added, "that if you saw how the German people put up with the death and destruction in their cities—you recall what Gerrit and Jan have told us?—you would wonder where they got their fortitude. And they are not a churchgoing people. I can't help admiring them. Yet..."

"I can't help feeling that the war will be won by the side with the biggest armies and air forces," said Bert.

"So it doesn't seem to matter in this war whether you go to church and pray or not."

"I'm getting a little tired of that refrain, Ria," Mother retorted again, in admonishment.

"You'll understand when you're a bit older, Ria," Father explained.

"And I'm getting tired of that refrain," retorted Ria.

"Among other things, the Church teaches us to see ourselves as part of a larger picture, in which we do not feature as the principal actor. Each person eventually passes on, but we as a people, and our Church, remain, and perpetuate our faith and our race."

"And not only remain," Father added, "but better for what each person has been able to give. When the Allies win this war and we have survived, we will owe it to some power greater than armies. It may be difficult to see that now, but when ..."

"When I'm older, you're going to say. I am now fifteen. You still treat me like a little girl. That was four years ago. Remember: I have just had to get photographed by the *moffen* for my ID card."

Father looked at Ria; then at Mother.

"You know, dear," he could not help admitting to Mother, "she is right..."

"You have grown up, it is true, but your situation has not changed, and we are still prisoners in our own land. You are still a young girl and we are your parents, and we have to look after you..."

Mother's wise admonition is interrupted by the sound of shooting. And once again the dreaded noise of shouting and running and loud stomping feet is heard outside. We all look at each other, half in fear, and half in the expectation of better news.

"I am going to turn on the radio," said Father, "and to damnation with the consequences!"

After the usual pause, the familiar BBC voice came across the airwaves:

> ... we cannot tell you more just now, than that the Allies have launched an assault by airborne troops against a vital strategic communications area, which, if successful, will materially shorten the war. Our next bulletin will be broadcast at six p.m. this evening. Goodbye for now. All will be well. Never lose hope. Rescue and liberation are near.

The noise of war began to come a little closer. Ria and Bert, looking at each other in great excitement, went rushing outside. After a few minutes, Ria came dashing back in.

"Papa, Mama, there are parachutists over Elst and Oosterbeek. Thousands and thousands of them. They're the Allies. Our prayers are answered. We're liberated! Oh, joy! oh, happiness! I want to sing and dance! Come and look, Papa!"

No sooner had Ria rushed outside again than Mother urged Father to go and look too. Father needed no further bidding. But hardly had he stepped outside and looked about him than what he saw alarmed him beyond belief.

"Ria, my child, what are you doing on the roof? You must come down this instant! Do be careful. Bert, are you up there too?"

"Yes, Papa. It is really quite safe. At least, it's safer here than at the end of those parachutes. Do come up. You should see the parachutists ... thousands of them, to the west of the city. And hundreds of planes and gliders and transports ... And oh, just look at all those fighter planes! And not a single German in sight! I've never seen anything so thrilling...!"

Mother joined Father and looked up. Her face lit up. Then she said something inaudible and re-entered the house.

"You must come down now, Bert. We must go back to church to give thanks. Tell Ria. We will listen to the radio later."

"We are not going to church. Ria and I are staying here to watch. We're being liberated. This is far too exciting. Ria and I wouldn't miss this for anything."

A short while later Mother and Father emerge once again, accompanied this time by Ina, as they prepare to set off for church.

Hardly had they left when Jan came down. He was soon joined by Bert and Ria, who had seen enough for the time being.

"Jan," said Bert, "your timing was perfect! You have got home just in time for our liberation."

ARNHEM PARACHUTE DROP

XIV.

Mother is busying herself in the kitchen as usual, trying to concoct something appetizing out of odds and ends of food that is becoming increasingly scarce. Occasionally she looks up, in the direction of the sound of sporadic gunfire which penetrates into the house through the walls and windows.

It is a beautiful, warm and sunny day, but no one in this Holland of ours which is still occupied by the hated enemy can be anything but a prey to a solemn foreboding and sadness. Mother's features, which appear the personification of glumness, can be taken to represent the mood of all the unliberated Dutch people.

A little time later Father comes into the kitchen, wiping his hands on a cloth. Mother looks up at him, tries a half-hearted smile, gives up, and turns back to her work.

"I fear the worst," says Father. "I'll see if there is any news on the German radio."

He goes over to the speaker in the corner and switches it on. At once a gloating voice is heard:

> ... our victory is complete! The Allies have been hurled back with tremendous losses. Theirs was a bold and daring stroke indeed, the attempt to capture the Rhine Bridge at Arnhem, which would have given them control of the undefended plains of Northern Germany and led them to Berlin. But ours was an even bolder stroke. Whereas the enemy succeeded in

capturing the bridges at Grave and Nijmegen, we out-manoeuvred them at the strategic fifth bridge and annihilated their whole army...

Father switches off the radio in disgust:

"I don't believe it! It's Nazi propaganda! We'll get the truth from the BBC."

He goes over to a bookcase, discloses the secret panel, which he opens to reveal the hidden radio. As he switches it on, the four of us youngsters troop in, and after a minute this English voice comes across gloomily:

... the Allied soldiers at Arnhem fought heroically, outnumbered as they were by five or ten to one, and running short of ammunition, until they were forced to surrender, the gallant few who were not killed or injured. Theirs was a feat of arms which will forever be celebrated in the annals of war...

Father switches off the radio.

"The British always seem to delight in extolling their defeats," he observed with uncharacteristic acerbity, "and in making of them episodes of tactical brilliance and heroism. First Dunkirk; then Singapore; next North Africa. Now Arnhem."

Ria looks crestfallen and says with dismay:

"We've lost, haven't we?"

And Ina bursts into tears:

"Oh, My God! Now we'll never be liberated, will we?"

Jan intervenes, trying to look on the bright side:

"Aren't you forgetting the Battle of Britain? But for that victory there would never have been a Second Front."

There is no arguing with the fact of the defeat, and the loss of hope, for what seems to them for another protracted period. Father recovers his *sang froid* and says:

"I was a bit hasty. After all, the Allies have liberated most of Holland..."

"... and (added Bert) they are only fifteen kilometres away, at Nijmegen."

"Yes, that is so," said Mother. "Shall I brew a pot of coffee? Which blend do you prefer—ground acorns with roasted rye, or roasted rye with ground acorns?"

"How about ground acorns with roasted acorns?" suggested Bert. "Then we can keep the rye for a special occasion!"

*   *   *

The sound of troops marching by, of heavy vehicles and shouting fills the air, coming to a crescendo and then fading away. Ina and Ria cannot help cringing a bit, and cover their ears, while Mother comforts them.

Mother disappeared into the kitchen, followed closely by the girls, to see if they could help. Father, for his part, took Jan and Bert aside and told them, in gentle tones, that they were now young men, and must do all they can to support him in keeping up the spirits of their mother and the girls.

"It is true, as you said, that the Allies are only a few kilometers down the road. If things get bogged down during the winter, the Allies are bound to resume the offensive in the early spring, so perhaps our situation is not as bad as it could be, and ... Ah, here's the coffee..."

"Yes, here's the coffee, Willem, and I think you were about to add: 'such as it is' but thought better of it this time."

"Yes, my dear, I was, and I bit my tongue. No one can do better than what you have done all these years. But it won't last forever."

"You know," said Bert, "that might be quite a good motto for us: 'Such as it is !'"

"I can go one better," chipped in Ria.

"You always can! But let's hear it!"

"It sounds like a very good title for a song!"
Ria started humming, making up a tune as she went:
"Such as it is,
Yes, such as it is.
It could be a lot worse,
But we'll take it for now,
Such as it is!"
Poor Ria's lip quivered, and she burst into tears.

We all tried our hardest to cheer up, to a certain extent, and reassured each other that, after all, we would be liberated eventually, and at least we were all secure in our own house, even if some foods were running short. But the hope of imminent liberation, after four long years of Nazi brutality and atrocity, to be damned so swiftly and rudely, was a bitter pill to swallow. But Father was not to be defeated, and tried to give heart to us all.

"We are secure enough in our house, and I am sure we can last out another few months, until Spring, if necessary, for our liberation. And I am beginning to wonder already whether our 'friends' will be able to set up a secret link with our fellow countrymen a few kilometres away who have already been liberated."

We were beginning to feel a little more secure, perhaps even complacent, when, just two days later, we were alarmed one evening by a renewal of shouting, stomping feet, and all the signs of outrage. This was followed by a loud banging on our door; to be accompanied by shouting that sounded like: "**Heraus! Heraus!**" The banging went from door to door down the road. And suddenly again, our door burst open and two soldiers stormed in threateningly:

"**Heraus! heraus**! Everyone out onto the road and listen to the announcements."

The soldiers went around the house searching for people. Father went forward and confronted one of them:

"What do you want? What do you mean by '**Heraus!**'?"

"You are all to go outside and listen to instructions. How many of you are there?"

"We are six. My wife and ....".

"All of you: Out!"

The soldiers began pushing us towards the door, until our parents protested:

"All right, soldiers, you can be a bit civil, can't you? We're going."

"We know you're going, we'll see to it."

We found ourselves outside on the pavement, wondering what next. We were not alone: far from it: every house was soon emptied, and hundreds of people lined the road, all wondering and looking more than a little apprehensive.

Before long an Army truck appeared round the corner and headed very slowly down the road. It was surmounted by a large speaker. Almost immediately we all heard a message blaring from it:

. . . .
. . . .
. . . .

OR THE EAST. YOU WILL WALK AND TAKE WITH YOU ONLY WHAT YOU CAN CARRY.

YOU WILL ALL LEAVE YOUR HOUSES TOMORROW MORNING AT FIVE O'CLOCK. YOU WILL LEAVE ARNHEIM AND TAKE THE ROAD TO THE NORTH OR THE EAST. YOU WILL WALK AND TAKE WITH YOU ONLY WHAT YOU CAN CARRY.

YOU WILL ALL LEAVE YOUR HOUSES TOMORROW MORNING AT FIVE O'CLOCK. YOU WILL LEAVE

. . . .
. . . .
. . . .

As the vehicles disappeared down the road, leaving hundreds of citizens looking about, lost, bewildered, unbelieving, small groups slowly began to come together, seeking consolation, information, encouragement.

German troops followed in the wake of the trucks, bellowing orders, and threatening violence if we did not get back into our houses and get ready for our evacuation the next morning. They bellowed in the face of the citizens:

"Get back in your rat-holes! The enemy, your friends, are routed and captured! *Heil Hitler!*"

Father was not going to submit meekly to those terrorists. He went up to one of the soldiers aggressively and demanded:

"How can we leave in a few hours? It is preposterous!"

"It is not **preposterous**," he shouted mockingly. "It is war! It is victory! You will do what you are told. We are the masters! You have lost the war!"

"No! You spout lies! You have lost the war. The Allies are snapping at your heels. Tomorrow they will be at your throat! That is why you are frightened!"

"Me, frightened! We, frightened...."

The soldier raised his rifle as if to strike Father with the butt, but Father calmly stood his ground.

"That's right, brave soldier—hit a defenceless old man." Then, in a softer, placatory tone, he asked: "Yes, you are the masters—for the time being. But tell me, soldier, where are we to go?"

"I don't give a damn! Go where you like. Go to hell! But you will leave tomorrow morning at five o'clock!"

Mr Mollen grabbed the soldier, thrust his face in his, and said: "But where are we meant to go?"

The soldier thrust Mr Mollen away and spat:

"Take the road to the east. Stay off the main roads. And I hope you never come back!"[8]

---

[8] It remains a mystery to this day who gave the evacuation order. See Appendix A.

PART TWO
EVACUATION

INTERLUDE.

Get out a large scale map of The Netherlands. Look towards the north, and there, located in the central region of the country where it narrows markedly between Utrecht and the German border, you will see Arnhem.

The city of Arnhem is where the battle was lost, the fifth bridge over the river Rhine. But look again. Just to the south of Arnhem is the city of Nijmegen. Nijmegen, and all of southern Holland, has been liberated. But the north and the east are still occupied by the Germans. And will remain occupied until the offensive is resumed in the early spring of 1945. And to think that thousands of poor people in the regions of Holland still occupied by the Germans were to die of starvation in Amsterdam; and hundreds of thousands were to suffer cold and hunger throughout Northern Holland, because...because of what? Well, we needn't go over that again.

But look still again—look at some of those thousands of people. You see them down there? They come plodding their sorrowful way out of Arnhem, and all the many surrounding towns and villages, to an unknown exile.

It is only five o'clock, but it is already lightening in the East. We cannot count them, but we know they number over one hundred thousand souls. Where will they all go? Where will they find shelter?

Already, since three o'clock this morning, people have been coming out of their comfortable homes and striking out east and north—although 'striking out' is altogether the wrong image, and conveys the wrong impression of people intent on reaching a known goal.

For in the beginning, with so many thousands of people taking to the roads, progress was slow. First, of course, there were many elderly people, and many children.

In fact, nearly all of them are children and youngsters and their parents and grandparents, for the able-bodied men aged eighteen to forty-five had been sent to Germany and to the conquered countries of Eastern Europe to work in the factories, and mines, and mills, and shipyards.

Then again, with so many hundreds and thousands of people crowding the roads and streets together, they were bound to get in each other's way a bit. But it will be noticed that they do not get angry or short-tempered, for they recognize that they are all in the same boat.

Then again, they are encumbered with necessary, or valuable, possessions. They pull or push all sorts of wheeled conveyances, from prams, to wheelbarrows, to small carts, all loaded with food and bedding and clothing, and anything that the owners think would be necessary to them in their exile.

They make very slow progress, in fact. But then, they are not in a hurry! Their major concern is to find someone hospitable enough to take them in. Some few are fortunate in that they have a relative or good friend not far beyond the limits of the evacuation area. For assuredly the news of the mass evacuation would spread like a spring wave on the ocean, and people with a room or rooms to spare would open up their houses to the unfortunates.

But what if you are a large family of six, or eight, or even more members?—who would have spare accommodation capable of housing so many?

Gradually, slowly, little by little, the mass of people, all starting out from a small number of central points, of which Arnhem itself is by far the largest—all these people, as they trudge along, find themselves fanning out along the roads. Quite literally: for, the farther they walk away from the starting-point, more roads open up before them; and the sheer numbers begin thinning out, so there is more room for all, and therefore more houses and farms where shelter might be found.

On the first day progress is painfully slow. But bit by bit the going becomes easier; so that on the second day, and especially on the third day, families and small groups even find themselves alone. That is what our family experienced. Let us look for them.

ARNHEM EVACUATION

Adjusting the zoom-lens of imagination, we scan the scene and picture to ourselves the route they would have taken. So we survey the road leading to Didam. Still too many people! We wait until well into the second day, and cruise the roads leading out towards Loil and Holthuizen, and Wehl. No luck! On the third day, *voilà*! we pick them up finally. They have reached Meerenbroek, and they are making good progress. All along the road they make inquiries. Their best chance is to find a large house, either empty or with but one or two occupants, or a farm.

They reach De Huet. Evening is approaching, and it is clear they are getting tired, and a little discouraged. They are approaching Doetinchem, and Ina is beginning to wilt.

"Mama, I'm so tired!"

"Yes, my dear. Just a little bit longer and I'm sure we'll find somewhere,"

"We've been walking for three days now..."

"Look!" exclaims Ria suddenly. "There's a farm over there! ..."

"You're right," replied her father. "I'll go and inquire."

While he was gone they sat down and waited. Bert wondered out loud:

"Whatever could have happened to Marie and her parents? They were with us until yesterday."

"Don't you remember, Bert? We got separated when the police herded us in different directions."

"I'm sure Gerrit will find out where they went and let us know where they ended up."

The family had not to wait long before Mr Mollen returns with another man.

"Look! They're going to take us!"

Ria lets out a whoop of joy, not diminished by the obvious element of relief in her exclamation, and danced a little jig in the roadway.

"It does seem that way," added Mrs Mollen.

"This is Mr van d'Berg" said Mr Mollen by way of introduction. And he proceeded to introduce his family. "Mr van d'Berg is kindly going to allow us to stay in his barn. More than that: to make it our permanent—or I should say: 'semi-permanent'—home for as long as the war should last. I cannot thank you enough, Sir, on behalf of all my family."

"Are there any cattle or sheep in there?" asked Ina plaintively.

"Not a chance!" replied Mr van d'Berg. "I only wish there were. The Germans took them a long time ago. The barn is empty. Come and have a look at it. It was built in the eighteenth century, and is of very solid construction. I am sure you will be able to make yourselves comfortable."

Ina sidled up to Jan, Bert and Ria, and expostulated mildly: "A barn! How can we live in a barn?"

"Well, you can always sleep outside!"

"Come and meet Mrs van d'Berg. I think she is preparing some hot soup for you."

The family follow the farmer into his home, and they repeat the introductions when they meet Mrs van d'Berg.

She leads them into a spacious kitchen. In the centre is a large wooden table. She clears the few things from it, and quickly lays eight places. Chairs are brought, all seat themselves where they please, and the soup is served, with generous slices of home-baked bread.

The Mollens and the d'Bergs exchange their views of the general situation, how they have coped under the hostile occupation, and the prospects for the future. They share the opinion that the war could not last much longer, but that much depended on the weather the coming winter. Food was already running short. The Germans had stolen everything they could. And it would come down in the end to everyone fending for himself—without, however, it being at the expense of one's neighbour. All must help all. With that, they got up to inspect their new quarters.

"We will give or lend you what we can spare for your immediate needs," explained Mrs van d'Berg.

"For the rest, you will have to see how the Red Cross can help. There is little to be bought."

Mr and Mrs Van d'Berg led the way to the barn, and let them look around and explore its possibilities. They set to at once to rig up temporary compartments for sleeping quarters, by means of poles and twine and curtains, for the parents, the girls, and the boys. That done, they turned their attention to 'beds'. The sole solution that the hosts could come up with was lengths of material and spare sheets, which they basted together at one end and at the two sides, and filled with hay. For covers and pillows, they used their clothing.

And so passed the third day of their exile, and the first-night of their new 'home'.

I.

Our parents were awake and up early the next morning. They couldn't sleep. Their minds were beset by a multitude of thoughts and feelings and fears and worries. Not so much on account of themselves, as on ours, their children's. That is what parents are like.

They were prepossessed with concern for the welfare of us, their family, in the material sense, which is often enough readily catered for; but even more worryingly for our mental, or spiritual, condition. Yes, our state of mind. How would we be able to cope with these basic conditions that we were thrust into?

To be uprooted from a happy and comfortable home and cast into material conditions such as these were was one thing; but the uncertainties surrounding their new life is another, and worse.

Our parents had already reconnoitred our new home, and ascertained at once that there was a pot-bellied stove in the barn—what a blessing!—and a small store of wood. Of dry wood at that!

Ria complained that it took her ages to fall asleep, saying she was too tired to sleep.

"Nonsense! I checked you twice. You were sleeping like a rose!"

"And Ina slept like a log!" added Jan

"Mama, don't let Jan pick on me!"

"No one is going to pick on anyone."

"I hate it here! I think I'll die!"

Mother was sympathetic, without being indulgent.

"We all hate it, my dear. We cannot change it, so we have to learn to put up with it, and be brave. Now let us have breakfast."

During their meal Father announced that he would go and talk to Mr Van d'Berg and find out how he can help us to make this place as liveable as possible.

"That will take a miracle!"

"Well, Ina, we may find that miracles still happen!"

"For example, shelving, and cupboards, and closets. Yes, and a table and chairs. That's for a start."

They had hardly finished when there was a knocking on the door.

"Jan, do see who it is."

Jan went over to the door, accompanied by Bert, and came back with Mr Van d'Berg.

"I came to see how you were doing. You must have been through some bad times, and we want to do what we can to help you, but our resources are limited."

"Yes, it is kind of you, and we appreciate your concern. Perhaps, to begin with, since autumn and winter are approaching, you can tell us where we can get fuel for the stove."

"I'm afraid the supplies of wood are limited to what you can find in the woods around here. There is no coal or coke. And please don't burn the roof beams—until you are quite desperate!"

"And food?"

"What you can barter for in town—for as long as it lasts. And no one can tell how long, or short, that will be. Oh, that reminds me. I can let you have a carbide lamp.[9] It is up to you to buy fuel for it, if you can find any."

---

9   This lamp used calcium carbide for fuel. A reservoir was filled with water, and its drip onto the chemical was precisely adjusted. The water reacted with the carbide to produce hydrogen gas. When lighted, the flame produced an intense glow in a tungsten element, which was dispersed by a reflector. The light illuminated a fair area of the barn and was bright enough for reading .

In a word, they would be on their own from now on. And God be with you!

"Oh, by the way," he said. "I should warn you—and you probably don't need warning—that the Germans are everywhere. There are streams of them either going up to the front or coming back. And the Gestapo are apt to stop and challenge you at any moment."

Father saw our host out, and we turned to our tasks.

"The first thing we have to do is to see what we have brought with us. That will give us an idea of what we will need to look for next."

"I know what I have to do first," Father announced. "I have to go into town and see the bank manager. And look around at the state of supplies."

Then, to Jan and Bert:

"Do what you can in the meantime to make the place habitable."

* * *

Father left without further delay for town, a walk of three kilometers. His first visit was to the local branch of his bank. All accounts had been frozen by the Germans! He insisted on talking to the manager in private; and when Mr Mollen presented his passbook, which showed a very substantial balance, he was allowed to withdraw one hundred guilders.

"I'm afraid, Sir," said the manager, "that is the maximum amount I can advance. As it is I may be called upon to give an accounting, and I dread to think what will come of that. I know we must all help each other as much as we can in these terrible times, but the defeat at Arnhem makes things fraught with danger. Please don't come back for more. I will just have to refuse—unless you can obtain authorization from the police. Good day, sir!"

* * *

He began his walk 'home'—back to the barn—slowly, and pensively.

He took pleasure in the walk, and—yes! and in being alone, to collect his thoughts.

It was with great luck that he had found a store with a small remaining stock of calcium carbide for the lamp.

He had also managed, with great difficulty, to buy a second-hand axe. All such potential weapons were forbidden by the Germans, and they had long been handed in to the authorities, under pain of severe penalty—which amounted to deportation, and reduction to slave labour.

The axe in question had been hidden all these years by the store-owner—in case of need. He no longer saw a need for it; but Mr Mollen impressed forcefully upon him his family's need, if they were to survive the war. He was made to pay a stiff price for it.

The axe was carefully wrapped in strong brown paper. He carried it, not over his shoulder, as a woodsman would have done, but over his arm, as if it were an umbrella. From time to time he would hold it by its business end, and walk with it as if a walking-stick. But that way it was too cumbersome. He would have liked to carry it exposed and naked, over his shoulder, like a knight of old. But the truth to tell, he felt anything but a knight, or a soldier, or ready for fighting. He had other things to do, and to think of.

If the coming winter turned out to be mild, his and his family's sole need was to obtain food. And even now, food was not plentiful. There was no meat, and no fish, in the shops. One could only hope that the harvests were good, and that they would be adequately supplied with vegetables and fruit and grain.

Let's see now: they were still in Gelderland, and Gelderland was a fertile and productive province. What if the harvest was poor, or the Germans stole everything?—as they were accustomed to doing—well, then, they would starve. And, if the Allies did not liberate them in good time, they would starve to death.

If the winter turned out to be severe, they would need a lot of wood for their stove. That meant walking for miles and cutting down trees, and cutting them up, and hauling them back to the barn.

And if they could not get fuel, they would die of cold.

It was all if, if, if...

Of necessity, they would live from day to day, while trying to anticipate the needs for the next week's meals. And they would only survive if they all worked together, and helped each other, and allowed for each other's frailties. And it was up to the parents above all to show strength and confidence and assurance. Nothing would undermine the children's ability to survive their conditions more certainly than any display of fear or wavering on the part of their parents.

He paused at this thought, and looked about him. Ah, I'm almost back. There is the barn. And I expect everyone is hard at work.

Yes—while I have been alone, and enjoyed being on my own. If being on your own is salutary for adults—and I must make sure that my wife also has time to herself—it is equally important that the youngsters should each have their private times.

When Mr Mollen entered the barn and looked around he was amazed at the transformation that had been effected in his absence, to make it slightly less uncomfortable, and forbidding, a 'home'. Why, they had even found a couple of pictures to hang on the walls. There was a bookcase; and, even if it was a bit bare at the moment—they had to forego that luxury, nay necessity, on leaving Arnhem, because of the sheer weight of books—it would not be long before it would be filled again. And there was no gainsaying it—reading would again become one of their main leisure occupations in the evenings. I'm not a great reader myself, he thought, but Mother and the girls will thank Heavens for the world of books—when they're not working their fingers to the bone!

The cart which they had wheeled laboriously for three days had been filled mostly with clothes, plus a little food and a few tools, and these had all been hung up, or arranged on shelves hastily, but firmly, installed on the wall closest to the area designated to serve as the cooking area, for it hardly merited the name of kitchen.

Then it was the turn of the two girls to bring out the possessions, mostly clothes, which they had brought. When all was set out there was a sudden scream from Ina. Ina stood there, as if transfixed, staring at her clothes. Among them was a row of shoes.

"I've brought six left shoes! How could I do it! I'm going mad!"

Jan was tempted to say: "You'll be walking round in circles!" but checked himself in the nick of time.

It was an occasion for feminine sympathy. Without hesitation, Mother took the distraught girl aside, and soothing her, said:

"That's all right, my dear. We will go into town right now and get you some good shoes. Don't let a little thing like that upset you. It could easily happen to anyone."

With Ina and her mother departed—with the parting admonition to see what else was available in the town, and accompanied by Ria—the three men set to work in the barn.

It was all of four hours before they got back. It is true, they lost their way for a while, on their way back. But they also happened to pass by the Church, and they could not pass up the opportunity to say a prayer. At least now they knew the way there when they were to go the following Sunday.

"We located the Red Cross in town," Mother announced. "They don't have everything we need but they can supply some of them, such as blankets. You might like to go in tomorrow and choose some. And we got two nice pairs of shoes for Ina. She is going to be all right now."

It was Bert's turn.

"There is a water-pump outside which gives good clean water. It appears it hasn't been used for years and we've got it working, thanks to a bit of oil that Mr Van d'Berg had to spare."

"That is good news! Perhaps we should have a cup of tea now, before we get back to work."

"Did we remember to bring some tea?" asked Ina.

"Yes, we did," said Ria. "Don't you remember? We wondered whether it was worth packing it, since it is only the leaves from rose hip trees."

"Oh, yes, that's right. And it makes quite good tea, *ersatz* tea though it is."

Mama added, for the boys' benefit: "I managed to find some potatoes and beans while we were on our shopping expedition. We're going to be all right."

II.

We settled into our new home – and hopefully our temporary home – as comfortably as we could make it. Our parents had their own 'bedroom' in one corner of the barn; the girls had their own 'quarters' beside them; and the men shared the other corner, all sectioned off by sheets and curtains and occupying the end of the building.

Blessedly, the weather was moderate, so we needed fuel only for cooking. But already, in October, we felt that the search for food was going to prove to be a critical matter.

One day we heard via the grapevine that a farmer had a little extra milk to spare. Where was he? In what direction? Oh, beyond Zelhem, about ten kilometers away! Papa wasted no time in sending Bert and Ria on their way.

We had no maps, and if unsure of our route we had to ask the few rare souls we met. They would want to know what we were going for. We had to tell them; and invited them to go with us—we were all in the same boat—provided we spoke to the farmer first!

That sort of word got round quickly—or people were out on spec, for the farther we went the more we found ourselves amongst other, similar 'hunters'. On this particular day, we had only gone a further one or two kilometers, and found our route leading us down a long and exposed path with open fields stretching for several hundred meters on either side, when we were startled by the roar of aeroplanes. We looked up and in the direction of the noise, and suddenly spotted the fighter planes bearing down on us.

Bert and Ria looked at each other in alarm. Bert pointed hurriedly to the side of the road, and shouted:

"Foxhole!"

Ria darted across the road, saw the foxhole, and jumped in. She landed on something soft, as she had expected; but what she had not expected was that the 'cushion' she had alighted on would start moving. And not only moving, but uttering sounds!

"What the hell! Goddammit! Get off me, for Christ's sake!"

Ria heard a burst of machine-gun fire, and hunkered down even more closely on top of the now heaving mass beneath her. Finally the mass gave a great thrust, and Ria found herself propelled, willy-nilly, up and half out of the foxhole.

She scrambled to her feet and looked around: the planes had passed over and disappeared. She looked down into the foxhole, and witnessed the sight of a large man trying to stand up, and somehow striving to maintain the figure of a man, and the dignity of a man.

He clambered out, stood up. It was difficult not to feel a little sympathy; and even harder not to laugh. He was covered from his waist down with soft, liquid mud.

By now Bert had re-joined Ria and they stood side by side surveying the sad spectacle. The man was wiping the mud off as well as he could, looking around him, and muttering obscenities under his breath. Ria could not refrain from saying:

"I'm so sorry, I didn't know you were there."

"And what if you had known?" he spluttered.

They watched as the man wandered off.

"You know who that is, don't you, Ria?" asked Bert.

"No, should I?"

"It's Mr Keegstra the city councillor who's suspected of dealing on the black market!"

"Oh, then I'm glad I jumped on him!"

"Well, let's go and look for our generous farmer."

Bert and Ria continued their search. Reaching the end of the long dike the country opened up on all sides ahead of them, and they spotted farms scattered here and there. Already a few people were to be seen approaching them, on the same quest. Bert and Ria selected a more distant farm which had not yet attracted any evacuees.

They walked up the pathway, knocked on the door, and did not have long to wait before a kindly-looking woman in her fifties opened the door. Bert explained our need. She was sympathetic, but warned that she would not be able to provide for much longer.

"I can give you a litre of milk, and I'm afraid that is all. Do you have a bottle?"

She went back into the house, and returned shortly with the milk. Bert offered her some money.

"No, I don't want any money. I can't do anything with it anyway." She added, meaning to be helpful: "Not everyone round here has anything to spare, and the food situation is sure to get worse. You cannot expect a warm welcome from many farmers."

When Bert and Ria got home with their offering they were greeted with an effusion of thanks, as if they had found a pot of gold. They told then of their adventure with the fighters, and the comic conclusion involving Mr Keegstra. Father and the boys had been out in the woods and brought back a substantial supply of wood, but the task had taken hours of searching.

III.

One day, shortly after we had established ourselves in the barn, we received a totally unexpected visit from Gerrit. As it happened, it was on a Friday evening and we were all at home. The questions poured out of us like water out of a burst pipe. We didn't notice it at the time, but Mother and Father just sat there, almost nodding knowingly, and as it were enjoying the exchange.

"How did you find us?"

"How on earth did you know where we were?"

"Who is your astrologer?"

"Why don't you just think for a moment?" Gerrit replied. "Do you think it was the Germans in their usual concern for the families of their conquered peoples who told me?"

"Wait a moment!" It was Bert who spoke. "You work for Herr Oldenkott. He is very influential ..." Bert's train of thought trailed off. Ria picked it up:

"Someone managed to telephone Mr Oldenkott's office. After all, his plant is at Oberhausen, which is not very far from here ..."

The links seemed to connect; and all eyes turned towards Father. Father sat there and smiled.

"Not only that," he explained, "but I also gave them the licence number of Rudy's truck, and they said they would do their best to locate him and give him our message."

"One blessing is," added Mother, "that, as we know, Rudy's work lies entirely in the area of Germany close to us here; on the other hand I am frightened most of the time because that is in the Ruhr, where the Allied bombing is most intense."

"So we should expect to be seeing Rudy as well fairly soon?" chipped in Ina. "Do you know whether Herr Oldenkott's office has managed to contact him?"

"I have no idea," answered Gerrit. "It is strictly business between us. Well, almost ... He wouldn't tell me if he had. On the other hand, he is a very nice man, and attaches a lot of importance to his Dutch ancestry. I'll give you an example. He has several plants; some of them are close to the border. There are two at Elten and Rees. Whenever possible he visits one of them on Friday so I don't have too far to go to visit you, and he will either stay there over the weekend or have someone come and pick him up from Oberhausen, and I will drive back there on the Monday."

"He certainly does sound like a nice man," said Ina.

"He almost makes you want to take up smoking," teased Jan.

The whole place was engulfed in a wave of excitement one day. Father and two of the boys were out on a foraging expedition, when, about mid-afternoon, with the rest of the family being at home busying themselves with various chores, Rudy burst in unexpectedly and told us to clear everything out of the front space of the barn

"I've got to go and find a butcher. Ma, boil up as much water as you can. Jan, here, I have a job for you."

Jan and Rudy left together; and the rest of us were left scratching our heads, wondering what Father was up to. We were soon to learn.

Jan was the first to return. He carried a ladder and a length of rope. Not long after there was a commotion outside; the door opened, and in came Father and Gerrit. Father was carrying a sack over his shoulder; and the sack was like a living thing, wriggling and squirming and writhing. And noisy! Suddenly it emitted a sound like a squeal.

"What's in that sack?" cried Ina. "You got an animal in there, haven't you?"

"Well, let's say ..."

"That's cruel! You must let it go!"

"And then starve?" inquired Gerrit, at once both soothingly and teasingly.

"I would rather starve! You're not going to kill it, are you?"

Mama came forward, took Ina by the hand and led her away:

"Go and put your coat on, Ina. We have to go to the shops. I've heard they have just got some soap in today."

Some time after Mama and Ina had left, Rudy arrived back with a butcher.

"This is Mr Mesman. He says he doesn't have much business these days."

Father and Mr Mesman conferred, and the butcher was asked what his fee would be.

"Money is of no use to me, so shall we say that we share the animal equally?"

All agreed that the butcher was a decent and honest man, and that they would be hard put to slaughter the animal themselves.

"We're all in this together. One half it is, divided equally."

The butcher nodded in agreement. He took off his coat and, opening his bag, pulled out his apron. He looked around and indicated the space where he would operate. He then prepared his equipment, which comprised: a hollow wooden pipe about a metre in length; a steel rod measuring a few centimetres longer that the pipe; a heavy hammer; an assortment of knives and cleavers and saws; and finally a basin.

In the meantime, while this preparation was taking place, Jan and Rudy were readying the ladder borrowed from our host.

Gerrit, on a signal, brought the wriggling, squeaking sack to the butcher, lowered it to the ground, and opened the neck wide enough to allow him to insert his arm. He rummaged around in the sack for a few moments until, having secured his grasp, pulled the animal out by its two hind legs.

"Hold it very firmly by the head," he instructed Gerrit.

"It's best if you get a lock on it between your knees. Yes, that's good. Now hold it still."

The butcher put the wooden shaft firmly against the animal's head between the eyes; he inserted the steel rod into the shaft and pushed it down until it came up against the head; then, picking up his hammer, and with a nod to Gerrit, struck the end of the steel with a sudden, sharp blow. The animal stopped wriggling, and went limp.

"Right, string it up here to the ladder by its hind legs."

That done, and the basin placed beneath its head on the ground, the butcher, with a deft and practised sweep of a large knife, cut its throat open. The blood poured out of the wound, and soon filled the basin. The bleeding stopped, the butcher ordered the animal down, and had it placed on the table-of-all-needs.

It was a fascinating spectacle, to see how he now literally butchered the pig, first slicing it exactly down the middle, so as to divide it into two equal parts, and then cutting up the two parts into its constituent sections, which he named as he severed them: ribs, cutlets, joints, hocks, etc. The organs he carefully extracted and placed in separate piles.

The work done, the butcher carefully packaged his share of the meat, packed up his equipment, and took his leave. Father and Gerrit, for their part, went about the business of wrapping and labeling and storing our share, while Rudy and Jan, without waiting to be asked, set about cleaning up. The only murmur of disapproval was vented when the butcher, taking up the basin of blood, asked where he could dispose of it. Dispose of it? What about making our famous blood sausage? Who, he asked, has the other ingredients? There was no answer: we had none.

When all was being restored to normal, Ria went up to Rudy and asked, "How much, I wonder, did Pa have to pay for that pig?"

"Have you," he answered, "ever heard the expression: 'Casting pearls before swine'?"

"Of course..."

"In this case," he added enigmatically, "it was a matter of casting pearls *for* swine!"

At that moment, Father happened to hear Rudy; and, grasping him firmly by the arm, pulled him over to one corner and spoke to him sternly. When released, Rudy made for the door; but Ria, intrigued, ran after him and asked what that was all about.

"Never mind, Sis. I'll tell you some day, but not today."

IV.

Fuel for the stove was a perennial, and growing, problem. We were having to go farther and farther afield to find any suitable wood. The local farmers were, understandably, unable to share with us intruders much of their limited supply. There was no electricity and no gas. All had been cut off, being requisitioned by the Nazis for their military and other needs.

The Germans added to the difficulties we faced, for they were swarming everywhere, and constantly stopping us in the streets to demand to show our passes; or even invading our barn without warning, or provocation, on random searches for... well, who knows what? They would find someone, or something, which would give them sufficient–and totally arbitrary–cause to march anyone off for interrogation, or confiscate anything for their own use. There was no appeal. And, of course, no possible chance of objection or refusal or resistance. Their weapons of destruction were their sole argument and justification.

One day—it was a rumour: maybe a rumour concocted for the purpose of giving heart to us captives—a goodly number of our fellow-Dutchmen were out foraging when, walking along a long dike, similar to our experience with the man in the fox-hole, a couple of Allied fighters came 'out of the blue', as the expression goes, and began firing. Everyone scampered for cover except for two German soldiers who were patrolling the dike. In a gesture of defiance, they stood their ground, aimed their rifles, and fired at the fighters. When the fighters had passed and dust had cleared, the local people, emerging from their cover, found two dead German soldiers, their bodies riddled with bullets, and not a single casualty among our people.

Whenever an event took place that was detrimental to the German war effort, no matter how small, the Germans went on the rampage. A perennial problem the Germans had was a shortage of manpower. Every able-bodied man was called up for the military. The occupied countries, especially those of Eastern Europe, whose people were deemed to be racially inferior to the Germans, were scoured for slave labour, and their men and women both were set to work necessary to the German war effort. In Western Europe, young men were put to work on local tasks.

So it was that occasionally there would be a round-up. This happened shortly after the Day-of-the-Pig. A small squad of uniformed men stormed in and demanded to see our papers. When we gathered with our papers, their boss went straight to Jan.

"You! Come with us!"

"What for? I've been evacuated from Arnhem and ..."

"Ah, yes, Arnhem. Ha! Because you lost that battle. Come! Work!"

Poor Jan had no choice; and to argue or question would provoke a violent reaction. It had happened before, at home, before our evacuation; but then there was no one of an age to be dragooned into work. Jan, on the other hand, was old enough. As it happened, on this occasion he was back later that same day. He had been made to dig ditches. In a way, he was lucky not to be deported to a slave-labour camp, in view of his earlier experience.[10]

---

10 The Germans who did this kind of work were called the **Organisation Todt**. It was responsible mostly for major engineering works, but also for building air-raid shelters and other minor jobs as needed.

TODT ORGANIZATION FORCED LABOUR

During the day we didn't notice it; but at night, sometimes, we were awakened by the noise of trains passing close to our barn. By 'close', we mean something like a kilometre or so. At night sound travels fast and seems clear.

We paid little attention to it, until one day, at breakfast, 'such as it was', Father raised the question in an almost haphazard way.

"Has anyone heard trains passing nearby?"

"Of course. What of it?"

"How are they driven?"

"By steam, of course!"

"Yes; but how is the steam produced?"

"By heat, silly!"

"And how is the heat produced?"

We all looked at each other, and slowly the penny dropped.

"Coal!"

"How fast do you think the trains are travelling when they pass by, say, the Maartens' farm?"

"Difficult to say. Probably not more than about fifteen kilometres an hour. And there's a bit of a gradient at that place."

The Barn

"Precisely! You boys: draw up a plan to recover some of our stolen coal. At night."

For reasons none of us can now recall with certainty, the job was entrusted to Bert and Ria. We think it was because, at this time, with Rudy and Gerrit away semi-permanently; and Father, because of his age and position, could not be risked on such a hazardous adventure; and Jan was under orders to be available for labour at any time. So Bert and Ria, despite their youth, had to chance their arm on it.

We spent some days and nights, for a whole week, keeping a log of passing trains. It became clear that trains passed in both directions at regular intervals. We had to determine whether they were troop trains, munition trains, freight trains, or passenger trains. We decided we could tackle any train other than troop trains. But troop trains became unpredictable, whereas all others seemed to follow a regular schedule.

We hit on a mid-week night about ten days after our discussion. We, that is Bert and Ria, set out at midnight, and had soon covered the distance to the rail track. Our timing was good: we had been there no longer than ten minutes when we heard a whistle in the distance. We chose a spot half way along the slope of the track. Soon the train came into sight. It was travelling very slowly. What a blessing! When the locomotive came alongside our position, Bert got up and ran beside the tender. We saw with joy that it was full of coal. In a second he had got a hold on a rung of the steel ladder fixed to the side of the tender and jumped up onto it. He climbed quickly to the top, and, standing on top of the mountain of coal, began throwing lumps of it down. When he had thrown down a good twenty lumps of varying sizes, he slipped easily down the ladder and jumped down on the side of the track. Ria was already busy collecting the coal in one of the sacks we had brought. We filled each sack, which was as much as we could carry comfortably; and collected the rest of our 'contraband' and hid it in small piles in places unlikely to be discovered, but easy for us to find again on subsequent nights.

The sacks were heavy, and we had to rest frequently; but the greeting was well worth the effort when we got home, apart from the extra warmth it would provide on cold days.

When we were not out foraging and scrounging, or trying to buy things needed, especially food and clothing, we would sit around 'at home', as comfortably as possible, between meals, or between supper and bedtime, and occupy ourselves with necessary tasks. These involved mostly the making over of clothes, or sewing of new ones.

This work fell to the women. They discussed their visit to the Red Cross in town. But the Red Cross was becoming increasingly short of the kinds of things we needed. They had, for example, kitchen items like can-openers and corkscrews. But who had tins or bottles anymore? If only! They had frying-pans, but who had anything to fry?

What they did have was books; and we made good use of them. During those long winter months, in the evenings, we beguiled our hours with reading. And when the light failed, or we had to economize on the fuel for our lamp, we would discuss what we had read in the semi-dark for a while before going to bed.

Father was not a reader—he had never had time in the past; and now that he had more leisure he found he could not develop the skills needed for it. He never ceased puttering around, fixing this and adjusting that, to give useful or necessary things yet a few more weeks of life.

But when in the late evening the light failed for working in or he ran out of materials, he enjoyed listening to our discussions. He never took part or commented, for, as he said, how could he say anything of use if he had not read the book in question?

Of course, if we were discussing a book which treated of a theme or event with which he was familiar, he might volunteer an opinion if pressed.

One such occasion arose when Mother had borrowed and read a book entitled *Gods gunsteling*. This was a strange book in more ways than one. First, it was written by a Dutch writer called Maarten Maartens. But Maartens wrote in English, and the book had to be translated into Dutch. Then there was the title: the original English title was *God's Fool*. But the Dutch word *gunsteling* did not mean 'fool': rather, it meant 'favoured one'.

The plot was equally strange. It tells the story of a nine-year old boy, Elias Lossell, who was rendered blind and deaf in an accident. He was somehow made the heir to his father's prosperous factory; but his two brothers, who envied him, quarreled, and one in an argument killed the other. Elias confessed to the crime; and the story ends inconclusively.

Mother said that she understood it perfectly. We children tried in turns to read it, but could not get very far before giving up; and for the life of us we couldn't understand a) why Elias should confess; or b) what the author as trying to get at. Mother explained that the whole story was, as it were, a commentary on I Corinthians 3:19, which reads: "For the wisdom of the world is folly in God's sight."

Mother must have been very discouraged by our inability—or was it a stubborn refusal?—to understand what she claimed to see so clearly. The story represented starkly, she insisted, the situation in which we found ourselves.

"It seems to me," she said, "that only a Christian could have written the book, and only a Christian can understand it. Who knows what lay behind the confession of Elias? What if a murderer went free? Only God can see into the hearts of men. And there will be a Day of Judgement."

Our discussion ended as inconclusively as the book. We couldn't rid ourselves of the suspicion that Father, who really was not a good churchgoer, sided with Mother for diplomatic reasons. And also to forestall any possible outbreak of animated opposition on our part... After all, was the author really intimating that we should not judge Hitler either, but leave him to God's judgement? The whole idea was quite preposterous!

"All is going to turn out well in the end," Mother assured us. "We will survive, and survive as a family. I know that God is watching over us, and will bring us safely out of our..... our predicament. Just look at Jonah, swallowed by the whale, and brought safely to shore! We are in a similar situation. Our barn is like the belly of the whale, which will keep us safe, until we come in sight of a safe haven again."

None of us had the unkindness to remind Mother that if God were so all-kind and all-knowing, He would not have permitted us to be thrown into such a 'predicament' in the first place. No, we did not argue with Mother. First, it would be pointless. We did not want to try to argue her out of her cherished beliefs because they gave her not only comfort, but the strength to look after us and care for us as she did. We, the rest of us, derived our belief in future liberation from other ideas or 'truths'.

When we say "the rest of us" we include Father. For we know that Father relied on Mother as much as Mother depended on us. We provided the material things necessary for bodily survival; Mother put them all together and, with the addition of her own invisible 'ingredients', transformed them into sustenance for the spirit. None of this is meant to downplay the role that Father played in our lives. We all felt that he too possessed the strength that would see us through any crisis. And we felt, too, that Mother and Father worked together almost entirely for our sake.

V.

Of all the chores that befell us girls, washing up after supper was the most disagreeable that we, Ina and Ria, ever had to do during the period of our evacuation. It is seldom that we had the luxury of hot water; and it was not long before we could no longer get soap. So we were reduced to cold water and soda. Soda was plentiful, and it was an efficient cleanser. But, then again, we had no rubber gloves, and soda is not kind to the hands. Woe betide you if you had even the tiniest scratch or chapping on your hands: it smarted! And the soda made the cracks in the skin worse.

We spent a lot of our time making over articles of clothing: pulling apart and re-doing into something still wearable. One of Mother's triumphs occurred during the cold spell which hit us later. We had managed to get an extra blanket from the Red Cross. Mother pulled it apart, and knitted thick socks out of the long woolly threads that resulted, with her wooden needles.

It must be said that Ina was not very good at sewing. But Ria made up for it. She liked sewing, even at that young age. It was a matter of grave regret that she was not able to bring their sewing-machine; but even so, with needles and what thread we could salvage or scrounge, she worked marvels altering and mending and making over many articles.

One event happened often, while we lived in the barn, but it will suffice if we tell of just one instance of it. We mean, when the German authorities demanded to see our papers. It was nearly always the Gestapo, of course, although we were only too aware of the ubiquitous presence of the soldiers, and, as we have seen, of other military or semi-military organizations.

One day there was a banging and hammering on the door of our barn kept up so insistently that the door was burst open. The Germans clad in long leather coats with swastika armbands, and pistols in holsters, burst in.

"Papers!" they demanded.

Only our parents were at home.

"Did you have to break the door down? You could have..."

One of the officers raised his arm as if to threaten Father. Mother tried, unsuccessfully, to stifle a gasp of horror and fear.

"That is not necessary, officer," she told them.

"Papers! And hurry up!"

"I will get them at once."

"You must carry them on your persons at all times. Get them!"

Mother hastened to her sleeping cubicle and came back within the minute with them.

"How many people live here?"

"We are a family of six. Ourselves and four children."

"Where are they?"

"They are all out looking for food."

"Why are they out looking for food? Why don't you grow your own food? Are you parasites?"

"That's a good question," added the other officer. "We have had a survey of the farms around here done, and the report shows only beets and rutabagas. Only animals can live on rutabagas. Are you animals?"

"We would like nothing better than to grow our own food, but it is winter."

Father would like to have added: "We will plant seeds next Spring, when you will have been driven out of our country,"—but discretion is often the better part of valour.

"Show me your children's papers!"

"But they have their papers with them."

"You had better be telling the truth this time. We will be keeping an eye on you. We have commandeered the house beside the farmer's and will be setting up our detachment there."

One morning—it was at the end of November—after what passed for breakfast, the farmer's wife called round and asked to speak to Ria privately. They went outside, and were gone a good five minutes. No one ever knew what they talked about. As suddenly as they had disappeared, they came back again. By that time the rest of us had made the necessary preparations, which consisted of one candle burning on the communal table. As soon as they reappeared, we burst out singing:

"Happy Birthday to you! Happy Birthday to you! Happy Birthday, dear Ria, Happy Sweet Sixteenth Birthday to you!"

We all went up and hugged Ria, who couldn't hold back a tear or two. Especially when Mother went to her and explained that we had no present—not this year.

Gerrit and Rudy managed to get away to visit us more frequently since we were evacuated, but seldom together. However, one weekend, shortly after Ria's birthday, we did have the pleasure of a joint visit.

They reported that life in Germany was getting more and more difficult even for the Germans, especially in the cities and industrial towns bombed heavily by the Allies.

Life was particularly harsh and dangerous for the men and women in the forced labour squads, who had to work in factories and mines. They had heard of the occasional attempt of sabotage, and theft or 'misplacement' of essential materials or components, and the punishments meted out to those caught—the Gestapo were not concerned about guilt or innocence—did not bear describing.

The two men went out that afternoon with Father to survey the surrounds, and to make a note of any significant changes or differences that had taken place since their previous visit. The brothers did not fail to notice the Gestapo office, thanks to both the ugly flag with its Nazi symbol of the hated swastika, and the vehicles parked outside.

When they got back home they were unusually quiet. And on one occasion they went into a private huddle with Father, and declined to say a word to the rest of us. Then they went outside and rummaged around in Rudy's truck.

The next morning, at breakfast, the conversation was especially animated, with everyone shooting questions at the two brothers, wanting to know in particular what they knew of the war situation, and when the allies were going to resume their offensive.

"The trouble is," said one or the other of us, "we can't get any news, and we all know how much trust to put in the Germans' announcements."

Suddenly Ina changed the subject.

"I don't know about the rest of you, but I hardly slept a wink all night. Did anyone else hear noises during the night? If we had an attic I would have sworn there were rats or squirrels scampering around overhead."

No one else claimed to have heard anything.

"Maybe it was spies on our roof."

Gerrit and Rudy looked archly at each other, smiled, and nodded to Father; whereupon Father got up, went over to a cupboard, opened it, and appeared to be looking for something. Suddenly the sound of music, of a piece of classical music, was heard very faintly. We listened in absolute silence, in total amazement, to this marvel. We all looked at each other, seeking an explanation.

It was Father who enlightened us—or, rather, who did not enlighten us. He simply said:

"Have a guess!" he teased.

"It must be a battery!"

"Yes, Gerrit has brought a battery from Germany."

"But," quizzed Bert, "we didn't know you had brought the radio with us?"[11]

"You don't!" said Father, in a non-explanation. "We will tell you all later, another time. For the meantime, you know enough now to never say a word to anyone about it."

Then, to Gerrit:

"Do you think you can get us some news?"

Gerrit went over to the cupboard, tuned in to the familiar wavelength of Radio Oranje, and then Radio Hilversum, but sadly there was no news of military action on the Western Front. But what we could not get by clandestine means we got from Gerrit and Rudy, precisely because of their work and contacts.

---

11   The Mollen family had secreted the radio in scattered parts amongst their clothing when evacuated. It came out later that, on the night in question, Gerrit and Rudy had strung up an extension from the Gestapo power line, which ran over the roof of the barn, through branches of trees, down to the barn, secreted between the walls. It was this walking on the roof in the middle of the night that had worried Ina.

VI.

There was no warning, no warning at all. Suddenly, on December 23rd—it is a date we will never forget—we all woke up to find ourselves encased in a deep freeze. From our secret radio we learnt that the whole of Europe had been engulfed in a weather system from the Arctic, which plunged us all, friend and enemy alike, in a bitter chill such as had not been experienced in Europe within living memory.

No one recalls now what we did that day. But on the next we all went out to look for fuel for our stove. This was to prove to be one of our two greatest worries in the days and weeks ahead.

This is the moment to record that every Saturday we were in the habit of taking our weekly bath. A large tub, borrowed from our host, was brought in; the boys boiled several kettles and pots of water, until the tub was half full; and the bathing began, in privacy.

The first to bath was Mother; then Father. After our parents we girls took it in turns, the oldest first; and then the boys had dubious privilege of bathing last, in water that was by then rather less than clear.

The following day, being Christmas Day, we all dutifully set off to church for the Holy Mass.

The sermon did not fail to dwell upon the Crucifixion, and the Salvation of mankind that it promised. But the church was like an ice-box, and if the good Father explained how we were to be saved, we were so intent on trying to ward off the cold, in one way or the other, that our minds failed to heed his message.

We arrived home and added as much fuel as we dared to our stove; and little by little we managed to coax a little warmth out of it. We had succeeded in hiding some of our 'liberated' coal, and this made a contribution to our comfort.

We were milling around, a bit aimlessly, wondering whether we should play a game, listen to the radio, or read, when Mother asked Ina and Ria to lay the table for dinner—for Christmas dinner, no less!

Thereupon, she left the barn. She came back in a few minutes, carrying something in a tray, covered with a cloth. We all sat down at the table, and Mother placed the tray in front of Father, who was waiting at the head of the table with knife and fork at the ready.

Mother, with a flourish, whisked off the cover, and there, lo and behold! was a ... a loaf of white bread!

Mother never did explain where she got the flour, and all the other ingredients; or what they cost in jewellery. But that bread was one of the most delicious meals of the war. It tasted like ambrosia—or what we imagined ambrosia tasted like.

Mother then, looking at her watch, announced suddenly:

"Why, I do declare that our Queen is going to broadcast at this hour. Do let us turn on the radio and see if we can hear her."

Sure enough, this is what we heard, which we thought must have been the end of her broadcast:

> The message of Christmas is not an appalling contrast to our present condition and our nameless suffering; the unfathomable and consoling love of Christ is there because of that suffering. Now that everything threatens to disappear and perish, it provides the only firm foothold among the shifting sands of the times. It enables us

maintain a courageous and convinced refusal in the face of the powers that threaten us with destruction, supported by God's supreme affirmation of life as it is laid down in this message; it confirms to us the eternal and imperishable existence of the 'Life' and the 'Light of the world', that St. John mentions in his gospel. The coming of that life, of that light in this world, means the fulfilment of God's promise to regenerate mankind. It is in Bethlehem that we all meet; that we all become conscious of the love that embraces and unites us all, as well as of the love for our fellow-men. That is where we learn what vocation means in our work, in our common effort for one supreme purpose; and it is where we see more clearly than anywhere else the need to put our success in this effort and the achievement of that purpose above everything else.

Christmas is the feast of promise: one of the things it promises us is a better future, which we may hope and expect to begin soon. This future will be founded to a large extent on our close co-operation in the spirit I just described. Nothing could be a better preparation for it than the Christmas message.

"Is that all?" asked Ina. "What does she mean?"

"Not 'she', my dear. The Queen, or Her Majesty, if you please!" scolded Mother.

"All the same, it's a bit rich coming from her, living in safety and in the lap of luxury," added Jan.

"If I know our Queen," explained Mother further, "she will not be living in luxury, but will restrict herself to the same rations that the British people have."

Father then took it upon himself to answer Ina's question.

"Would you rather that she say nothing, that she cease to broadcast to us?"

"No, Dad, that's not what I'm getting at. I do not understand what she said."

"Mother," said Father, "you can say it better than I can."

"As I understand it," Mother explained, "she was telling us what we all know but often forget. Christmas is also the message of Love, that bond of caring for each other that will ensure that we all survive this war, as a family and as a people, because it helps us to see our duty clearly. The Queen is telling us that she loves us as much as we love each other; that she thinks of us all the time in our plight; and that we must hold on and keep the faith, until we are liberated."

"Yes, my dear," said Father. "That is well said and how I understood her—the Queen's—message. We will hold on."

"It cannot be more than another month or two, at the most."

VII.

"Mama, I'm so cold!" It was Ina; and we all felt for her.

"I know, dear," said Mother through the curtain. "We all are. Just curl up and put your hands between your knees and try to think of having a picnic in the park. The night will soon pass."

It did, of course. But it was equally true that the cold often woke us up, and it was difficult to stop our teeth from chattering and our bodies from shivering. If anyone had kept a glass of water in the barn overnight, it was solid ice in the morning.

During the day the men went out in search of wood, as did all the other refugees. And so it was that we, and they, had to wander farther and farther afield, and often came back home with only a few sticks or branches. Once Bert and Jan found an old wheelbarrow in a ditch, and rejoiced, for while they glowed at the thought of the warmth it would provide if torn apart, they had a second thought, and used it to transport what wood they found, and decided to burn it only in an emergency.

If they passed a farm—and often they did—they stopped to ask for food or wood. And as the weeks passed, and the occupation became prolonged, some of the farmers became increasingly unwelcoming, or even hostile. We tried to appreciate their predicament; for they were daily besieged by many evacuees, and who knows whether they even has enough food for themselves?

One evening at this time our meal was the precursor of many a similar meal: turnips, nothing but turnips dug up in a neighbouring field. It must be admitted that Mother was not a good cook, but she did her sad best with what she had—with all that the rest of us could find or scrounge. And we were not surprised when, on some rare occasion, she could not help but let her normal equanimity slip a bit. Ria was obviously not enjoying the food, and Mama did not hide her disappointment:

"Ria, you're eating with long teeth again!"

"They can never be long enough," added Bert, with a glance at Ria. Ria simply grimaced, and shrugged.

Afterwards we all sat down and tried to figure out how far afield the evacuees had travelled from Arnhem—in other words, what was the geographical limit of the exodus—so that our men could go still farther out in the quest of food and fuel, where no other evacuees had bothered, or thought, to go. But there was no public transport: the buses had long ceased to run; and all bicycles, as we have seen, had long since been requisitioned. Or, as we preferred to say, stolen. Even if we had a bicycle, and dared to use it, it would have been taken from us within minutes, the presence of police and troops being so unavoidable.

Jan came up with the bright idea—well, it seemed bright when he first mooted it—that on Rudy's next visit in his truck, he could drive farther out into the country, farther than he had been hitherto, and perhaps find a generous farmer who had food to spare. But of course, we realized also that if he were stopped, far from his authorized route, he would be sent to a forced labour camp, with little chance of survival.

Another, better, idea was to suggest to Rudy that, on his next visit to us, he come by a different route, and pass through a part of Eastern Holland not reached by evacuees.

It so happened that his next visit occurred at about the turn of the new year. But before we had a chance to put this brilliant idea to him, he had a surprise of his own for us.

He placed on our communal table a largish rectangular object wrapped in brown paper.

"Guess what it is?"

We were not allowed to touch or feel or lift it.

"Bread."

"Soap."

"Gold."

"Wood."

"A pig!"

"You're all cold! Mother, you lift it and have a guess."

Mother picked it up, balanced it, squeezed it, and said:

"Cheese."

"Right!"

She unwrapped it, and there before our admiring eyes lay a slab of cheese weighing at least two kilograms. We all looked questioningly at Rudy.

"I was leaving a bombed-out food warehouse at Duisberg yesterday when I spotted it on the ground in its original wrapping. My guard had already left and was waiting in the truck. I hid it in my coat and threw it —not so hard!— in the cab of my truck when I got in. The guard didn't notice anything unusual. I dropped him off at the border, and here I am!"

"But where's the bread, Rudy?" taunted Jan. "We can't eat cheese without crusty bread."

"Well, maybe you can't, but everyone else can!"

We then changed the subject, and asked Rudy whether he had to cross the border into Holland at the same place, or whether he could come across at, say, Hengelo, farther north. We explained what we had in mind.

"I'm afraid not. My travel is very restricted, and controlled. I have to cross at the check-point closest to my family."

Well, that was that! It seemed a good idea; but often good ideas are like crystal streams which just run away into the ground.

The temperature had dropped to –27°C and even the ground was frozen hard. Yet food had to be found. And Father took Rudy out to see if they could dig up a few turnips. Mother thought a turnip dish with cheese sauce might be bearably palatable.

"A pity there's no pork left," said Ria. "Pork and turnips go well together."

"Anything goes well with turnips."

Rudy stayed the night, and the next day he and Father roamed far afield in search of wood, while Jan, Bert and Ria sallied out in the hope, a diminishing hope, of finding some food to barter for.

VIII.

It was during this mid-winter freeze-up that Ria began suffering from a severe toothache. For well over two weeks she said nothing about pain, but Mother began to notice a change in her. At first Ria began to go off her food; but this was put down to boredom with the same old fare, or the lack of flavour. Then she showed signs of tiredness, due to lack of sleep. Then again, she became irritable, and testy, and so different from her usual cheerful self. Finally, unexpectedly, at supper, she gave a yelp of pain which she couldn't suppress. Our parents forced her, with all the compassion in the world, to tell them what was troubling her. On her confessing *à contre coeur*, that she had had a toothache for two weeks, Mother managed to peer into her mouth, and detected a severe swelling and redness at the back.

She wasted no time in taking Ria into town in search of a dentist. After numerous inquiries they were directed to the only dentist in town who had not closed his practice, one Doctor Rore.

He examined Ria with the professional skill that comes of long experience, and announced the bad news, that one of the molars was severely infected and had developed an abscess. He was sorry, but he had no medicines to treat it with. The other dentists had closed their practices because they could get no medicines, and no x-rays, and no equipment.

Mother took in the implications of his remarks, and asked anxiously:

"And no anaesthetics?"

"I'm afraid not, Mrs Mollen."

"And the tooth...?"

"The tooth will still have to come out. I'm very sorry."

Ria was listening, and understanding, even with trepidation. Then, suddenly:

"Well, let's get on with it, shall we?"

Mother and the dentist looked at each other with utmost concern, and understood from their subsequent expression that they would have to act.

"I am going to have to strap you down in the chair, Ria," explained the dentist. "I cannot risk you moving suddenly. But before that I have something I want you to drink."

Dr Rore poured two ounces of amber-coloured liquid into a glass, added the same amount of water, and gave it to his patient."

"Drink this," he said. "It will help a little. Drink it fairly slowly, in small sips."

Ria took a sip, swilled it round her mouth, grimaced, and spat it out.

"Agh, it's horrible!"

"Do try again, a tiny sip at a time, and swallow it straight away."

Ria tried again, and eventually managed to drink it all, little though it was.

On then being asked, Ria placed her arms firmly along the arms of the chair. The dentist took two bandages from a drawer, and bound Ria's wrists to the arms of the chair.

Dr Roer then, asking her to open her mouth wide, applied his forceps to the tooth, and began to apply leverage. Mother told us later, with reluctance and after urging, that at first she tried to ignore the sound of the crunching of steel on bone , and the grinding of bone on bone, and then a sort of squelching and sucking sound, but those sounds are her sole recollection of the sorry event. Ria, for her part, did not remember hearing anything. All she remembered was the pain. It shot through her jaw and face like a bolt of lightning and filled her head.

She did not cry; but her eyes filled with tears, filled to overflowing with tears, which poured down her cheeks in steady rivulets. But Mother, though once a nurse herself and inured to the sight of suffering, could not stay a few tears. And I believe the dentist himself was not immune to a telling compassion.

The operation concluded, and the offending tooth discarded, Dr Rore undid the bandages which bound Ria's arms, probably unnecessarily, to the chair.

"Just rest a while," he said. "The pain should diminish shortly. You should lick the wound as much as possible, despite the unpleasant taste of blood."

The dentist explained further to Mother: "Everything should be all right now. It would be advisable if she did not to go out of the house for the next forty-eight hours or so, especially in this cold."

He did not accept a fee.

* * *

As if it had been a forecast, the weather got colder, if that was possible, and we all felt that we would never be warm again. If it was cold during the day, it was even colder at night. The Red Cross ran out of blankets, and we had to make do with what we had, and threw even our coats on top of us at night.

Hunger only added to our discomfort; yet it was essential to keep active, and to keep moving. Indeed, to stay at home and to try to kill time by playing games served only to lower our morale. To do anything, especially if it involved going out, whatever the pretext, helped at least to keep up our spirits. It also added to the impression that thereby we were hastening the passing of time, and the day of liberation.

THE HUNGER WINTER

The news we received on the radio was not uniformly bad—on the contrary, from the military point of view it was good. The Russian Army was penetrating farther and farther west, German cities were being progressively reduced to rubble by allied bombers; and in the Far East the Americans were recapturing more and more of the territories conquered by the Japanese in the early years of the war.

There was general alarm when we heard about the ferocious assault made by the Germans over Christmas and the New Year in a last gasp effort to drive a deep wedge between the American, British and Canadian armies. But this attack finally petered out, the line held, and the stalemate was resumed.

We realized that it meant at least another two months would pass before the Allies resumed their offensive in our sector of operations. Two months! How would we possibly survive another two months—another two months of cold and semi-starvation?

Yet there was one inestimable blessing we could count on—good health. We learnt from our radio that during that 'Hunger Winter', especially in the larger cities like Amsterdam, there were outbreaks of scurvy, of diphtheria, and of typhoid. And that many thousands of poor people died of starvation.

We were spared those calamities, and it is difficult to explain why we were spared them. It is equally difficult to say why we were never ill. For the fact is that none of us ever suffered from any ailment at all during that time: none of us ever had even a cold. A couple of humorists in the family were tempted to stress the beneficent role that the turnips played in our diet. In fact, we were forced to resort to tulip bulbs as well, and to beets.

On one occasion the men managed to dig through the frozen earth and recover a fair quantity of beets. We have mentioned that Mother was not a very good cook, and she was at a loss to how to cook them and make a tasty dish. We knew that beets were grown for making sugar, but no one knew whether they were a different kind of beet.

We had no ingredients with which to make the tasty hot beet vegetable served with a meat and potato dish. So Mother did the only thing she could, with the equipment we had. She decided to cut them up and boil them down into a soup. We wish she hadn't! The result, following prolonged rendering, turned out to be a thick, grey, gooey mess which we all found uneatable. Perhaps we should have cut them up and eaten them raw. How wise we are afterwards!

* * *

We have mentioned frequently that we were but one family among thousands who found themselves in the same situation as us, or even worse. How much worse it was for some we were to find out.

Most of us were out when it happened, on our daily excursions in search of food and fuel, and only Mother and Jan and Ina were at home that afternoon.

We were aroused from our work of fix-it and repair by someone tapping on our door. We looked at each other perplexed, until Jan took it upon himself to go and see who it could be. Obviously it was not the police, for they did not stand upon niceties—they simply burst in.

When Jan opened the door he was confronted by one of the most pitiful spectacles one could imagine.

Outside was a family of four—a mother and father and their two children. They were dressed, or rather covered from head to foot, in ragged clothes, and they looked drawn and exhausted.

"Please, do you have something to eat? We haven't had a crumb for two days."

Jan had no option: he invited them in. Mother and Ina came hastening up, and had them try to warm themselves by the stove.

"You poor dears," said Mother. "The very least we can give you for the moment is something to drink. Jan, go and get some water, please."

Jan promptly heated the reserve of water kept for the purpose, and took it outside to pour into and thaw out the water-pump. When Jan came back with water he announced that a plank in the siding of the barn was loose and it wouldn't need much persuasion to pull it out, and he disappeared again. Mother was already warming some water for our visitors. While they were recovering some of their little remaining strength, Mother and Ina set about the task of washing and cutting up the last of our turnip-tops. These they cooked into an edible state, and when done, they sat our guests down at the table. Mother served a portion to each, and then sprinkled a little brown sugar onto each plate. Ina finally she took out the remaining piece of Rudy's cheese and cut it into four equal pieces.

Our visitors were just about finishing their meal—'such as it was'—when Jan returned with some firewood. He was soon followed by the others, who came drifting back. Father was particularly proud of Mother, Jan and Ina for showing hospitality to the destitute family.

It was impossible to send them out again that night, and we had mother and daughter sleep in chairs while the father and the boy made do with a mat on the floor.

The next morning Father explained to the visitors that we did not have the room to enable them to stay longer, and proposed that we walk them into town and take them to the Red Cross, in the hope that someone there would be able to propose a solution to the dire predicament they were in.

So it was that we all set out, without breakfast—we pretended a glass of water was all we needed—and along the way we kept up as cheerful a conversation as we could. At one point the mother blessed us and said we would receive our reward in heaven—which prompted Ria to whisper to Ina that she would prefer to have it here.

On the way the mother, a young woman of about thirty who spoke well and who had, to put it mildly, seen better days, made a point of walking beside Father. She told him the saddest story we have ever heard.

At the time of the battle of Arnhem they lived in Rozendaal and had just been able to keep their head above water during the Occupation. Her husband could not work and was in a perpetual state of trauma. It happened when he was visiting his parents in Twente, in April of 1943. His visit coincided with the great strike that took place there. The Nazi authorities were ruthless, and to make an example to others they rounded up hundreds of the strikers and executed about sixty of them. Everyone was made to witness the shooting, and he saw his father shot in cold blood before his eyes. He has never been able to explain how he escaped and found his way back to Rozendaal; and since then he has not spoken much in the past year. Then came Arnhem and they were driven out of their home. He has been as dependent on her as the children are, and she has had to fend for them all. They tramped with hundreds of others, and just followed where they went. They slept in community centres, like others, for three or four nights, then just kept on walking the following morning. They had no idea where they were going, or what to look for. The streams of evacuees got smaller and smaller, until, one morning, they suddenly found themselves the only people walking. Where all the others had gone they had no idea. And they had no idea where they were. Whenever they came to a farm or a village the mother simply went to a house and asked to be taken in. It was not until the end of that day, the fourth or fifth day, when it was already beginning to get dark, that she prevailed upon a lady who lived alone to give them shelter. They were there very happy for about four weeks when calamity struck. Little Wim started wetting his bed at night. The mother did her best to cover it up but their hostess learnt of it and told them to leave. They went from one place to another, finding beds mostly in community centres, but they were never allowed to stay longer than three or four nights at a time. They started back-tracking, hoping to return to community centres they had stayed at before, but the mother lost her way frequently and they found themselves covering unknown ground and coming to different villages. Finally she threw herself and her family on the good graces and the charity of the pastor of a church—she discovered later that it was at Zelhem—and stayed for two or three weeks. Then suddenly he was arrested by the Gestapo, suspected of helping the Resistance, and the family were driven out, despite the pleadings by the mother. We have not been able to remember many of the details she told us, and we think that she has forgotten a lot herself. It must have been shortly after that that we came to their rescue. Or at least, gave them shelter for a night.

We had to leave the family at the Red Cross centre; we said our goodbyes and returned home. We are sorry we never learnt their name, and even sorrier that we never discovered whether or how they survived, when so many did not. We have often thought what a brave woman she was.

IX.

It seemed to last an age, the arctic blanket that enveloped us in a freezing block of ice and reduced life to a reluctant crawling pace that seemed to drag it out and out. From just before Christmas until the very end of January everyone was cold, cold, cold. It was perfect for preserving food, if we had had any. And the hunger that gnawed at us, shrinking our stomachs, only served to exacerbate the cold. It is said that shivering is Nature's way of preserving warmth, or of generating warmth, in the body. We would like to know that author of that theory, and we would have invited him to join us to put it to the test.

Weather is a strange, and little understood, phenomenon of nature. One day we were living in the North pole, the next day seemed like the south of France. Well, that is an exaggeration. But our ice-age ceased almost as abruptly as it had began, and the weather warmed up in ways that not only restored our bodies, but gave a lift to our spirits as well. Food, and hunger, now remained our chief worry—apart, that is, from the ever-present enemy.

We were encouraged to believe that the Allies would resume their advance against the Germans very soon, although we had no confirmation of that hope in the news we received on our wireless. If we had known that we still had to endure two months of occupation by the hated Germans, who became more nervous and unpredictably vicious as their defeat became more and more inevitable, we might not have been so sanguine. Not cheerful, no;

that was a state of mind, a luxury, that we never dared entertain. But an increasingly hopeful outlook, yes.

If only one could live on warm air and hope! We were, we dare say, even prepared to go so far as to eat grass, if it became a condition of our survival. That never became necessary; and none of us even went so far as to wonder what it tasted like, or how it was cooked so as to make it edible. But we came very close to it. The other aspect of the problem was that we would not even have known where to find enough grass for all!

During those next two months, food, and sheer physical survival, became our sole preoccupation. Had it not been for an occasional gift from heaven, as it seemed, we would have joined the thousands who did in fact starve to death in our country that year.

Every day, like a ritual, we sallied forth in every direction in the increasingly forlorn hope to find a farmer with an undiscovered cache of food. And almost every day we came back empty-handed. We did not know it at the time—our parents were careful never to tell us—but Father had bartered away all Mother's jewellery in exchange for food.

When we look back we can count our blessings in the shape of the beets and tulip bulbs and turnips that we did dig up. And that is especially true of the period that lay ahead, when the earth, now softened by the thaw, yielded its harvest more readily. We wonder, however, whether we would have all survived as we did, had it not been for the odd circumstance, as we have hinted. What we describe now is the most notable of the events.

It was late one evening, after curfew, when we heard shouting outside, accompanied by running. Even as Father went to the door to see what was going on, a man had banged on our door and, the moment Father opened it, he shouted: "Come quickly! Bring knives!"

Father needed no further bidding, and wasted not a second. As he picked up the largest knife that came to hand he called on Jan and Bert to follow. They ran outside and joined the few men already hastening down the road. Several had gathered only two streets away. What they saw was a horse, lying in the road, with an electric cable lying across it. Obviously the animal had been electrocuted—no one knew, or cared, how the German cable had come down. Jan and Bert joined two men who were already trying to drag the horse away from the cable without getting close to it. Having succeeded, the men, become instant butchers, set about the animal. Father carved off a very large portion of a haunch, and settled for that.

"We must let others have their share of it."

Within twenty minutes there was nothing left of the animal—hooves, head, everything was taken, to be put to good use—and the sole evidence of an animal's existence was blood and hairs on the road.

Fortunately we still had a little coal left from our second 'expedition of recovery'; but we had to avoid burning it at night lest the smoke give us away; and we always burned wood on top of the coal. We only regretted that we did not know, and had no means of discovering, the owner, if only to be able to share some of the meat with him.[12]

This whole episode raised a further issue which was vital to our survival, and which we had not talked about much, though we were aware all the time of its importance. It was, simply, information, and sources of information.

We happened to be in the right place at the right time to receive a piece of information which we regarded at the time, and which was confirmed later, as helpful to our survival.

We have made much of our success in concealing our radio. It was like a life-line. It is not realized until you lose a commodity how much you depend on it. We take too many of the appurtenances of life for granted.

---

12 Horse flesh was a common and accepted source of meat throughout Europe, so no one had any compunction in carving it up. They would certainly have done so in any event.

We grow up within a family, and a neighbourhood, and a larger community, which include school and church, and do not appreciate that they are sources of information which enable us to live in peaceful harmony with one another. Imperceptibly we attach a trust to the information.

As we grow up our horizons expand, and our appetite for information expands accordingly. Eventually, we need to know what goes on in the larger world which we cannot know personally—our province, our country, and even farther afield. For this we rely largely on remote and unknown sources of information.

Now another factor enters the equation, and may lead to wrong answers: Is the information trustworthy? How can one judge?

Before the war, the citizen was inundated with torrents of information, most of it slanted in such a way as to persuade the listener of its reliability. One of the principal aims of education is to teach the student the critical skills necessary for the formation of his judgement, and so to enable him to sort the wheat from the chaff, and to make allowance for the bias of partisan statements.

During the war, life in that regard was made simpler by far. We knew that, if the source of your information was a neighbour, a fellow-Dutchman, it could be relied upon, and acted upon. If it was the enemy, it was known to be slanted propaganda, if not outright lies.

But what of the progress of the war beyond our shores? It was precisely in order to learn the truth that Father attached an overriding importance to the radio, and took grave risks to keep and conceal it, especially when we were evacuated. Whereas Gerrit and Rudy were able to keep us informed about conditions in Germany, up to a point, for events on the Allied side we depended on Radio Oranje.

We learnt later that Father, also at considerable risk, was himself the source of information about the war for neighbours whom he felt he could trust. But as we have seen, those neighbours might themselves innocently pass on information to others—to others whose loyalty was not known for certain. Fortunately, the worst never happened.

Now, in those long-drawn-out months of February and March, our radio was of little comfort. We heard of the successes of the Allied armies in Italy; we heard of the massive victories of the Russians in the eastern front, which threatened to overrun all of Eastern Europe, and perhaps even, alarmingly, regions of Western Europe; and we heard of the amazing triumphs of the Americans in South-East Asia—which included our own Dutch East Indies, or Indonesia—in pushing back the Japanese closer and closer to their own homeland; and all that news was encouraging. But of our little corner of the world, and the prospect of liberation, we heard nothing. The allied campaign was stalled; there was no word of resumption; and our people were dying.

Every day, athirst for reliable information, we turned to the radio. We tuned in two, three, four times a day. Nothing. Or rather, every other part of the world except ours. Then, when we had reached a point almost of past hope, we heard that the Allies were on the march again, and that the town of Uedem had been captured. But Uedem was in Germany! We got out our precious map: there it was, a few miles south of Kleve, a large important town. The Allied army must have launched their offensive from the region south of Nijmegen, where they had been ensconced since September.

That was at the end of February. For a while after we heard no more news. Then there began what seemed like a thunderstorm gathering volume and intensity in the distance, and we, who hated the war with a passion, realized it was allied heavy artillery bombardment, and rejoiced. It was an unexpected source of information, this! and one which heralded the beginning of the long-awaited assault, and hope was rekindled.

PART THREE
LIBERATION

I.

As a family we followed with increasing excitement the military action and the progress of the Allied Armies' advance, thanks to our wireless and to the occasional careless word dropped by German soldiers, ever since the offensive was resumed in late February of 1945. We learnt that Uedem was liberated on February 28th; yet after that progress slowed, or came to a halt. We could only put it down to stubborn German resistance, although we knew that the Allies enjoyed an appreciable advantage in both men and *matériel*, and overwhelmingly in air power.

There was one thing, however, which told us unmistakably that the end was drawing near: it was bombardment by artillery.

It began with an air-raid on Doetinchem one night, and no one could figure out why Doetinchem, since there was nothing there of any military importance. Everyone finally put it down to an error: obviously some other target was intended, and the bombers' navigation and target identification were defective.

Then, early in March, what came to be called "drum-fire" began: heavy and constant shelling of enemy positions by Allied artillery. Like the good folk of Didam and Doetinchem, we tried to convince ourselves that we were not in any immediate danger, but in war, you know, all kinds of unpleasant things can happen. Many of our fellow-citizens, both near and far, were killed, but we accepted it as an inevitable and necessary cost of liberation.

The shelling went on for three weeks, and the nerves of people were beginning to get frayed. Our Ina, in particular, was showing the signs.

Fortunately there was an air-raid shelter close to our barn—in fact just across the road from us—and we took shelter there, by day or by night, when the shelling got particularly close or noisy. It was the basement of the community centre, converted into a shelter, and which accommodated a good hundred people, seated along benches on either side of the structure. It was a bit musty, and with only the dimmest of lights, but it was safe. Or at least safer than in the barn.

We were keeping a very wakeful ear open to the beginning and end of the bombardments which, admittedly, were sure to get on everyone's nerves and perhaps provoke short tempers.

It was lunch-time; breakfast had been a meagre salad concocted of any greens that could be scrounged from the fields, which, as everyone knew, were becoming increasingly raided and bare, as well as dangerous. People were lucky if they didn't trip or fall into a shell-hole. But there remained one field of crops, still, remarkably, yielding some turnips. But it was becoming increasingly dangerous going out anywhere in the open.

Mother was stoking the stove, and adding some of the last pieces of wood from our slender supply to keep it going just a bit longer.

"Jan," she called, "go and get me a pail of water, please."

"Yes, Mother."

"And tell Bert to go and dig up a few of those turnips."

"All right—but not everyone is going to be happy."

"I know what you mean. But, happy or not, it is that or starve."

Bert returned a good half-hour later accompanied by a German soldier. It was evident that the soldier and Bert were on amicable terms. Bert explained:

"This soldier is a cook. He and his unit are about to move on and he says he has a large bucket of soup left over, and he wants to know if we would like it."

In no time the soup was simmering away, the family had been called and introduced to their unlikely benefactor, and we all sat down to a bowl of the most delicious pea soup that we could remember having tasted.

The soldier obviously enjoyed himself in this appreciative company, and no doubt the first family gathering he had had the chance of in some time. On the other hand, he was not a young man, and probably a late recruit into the army. Eventually, it became apparent that there was a further reason for his tarrying, and delaying his leaving. He came out with a surprising request:

"Do you have a gramophone? I have found a record, and I would like to play it."

The soldier picked up his haversack and opened it, and after some careful feeling around, pulled out a record. It was a ten-inch bakelite record in only a paper slip-case.. It was a marvel that it hadn't broken.

"I have taken very good care of it," he explained.

"I will go and ask Mr Van d'Berg if he has a gramophone," offered Father; whereupon he got up and left. In the meantime the family cleared the table and began the washing-up. In short order Father returned with our hosts, carrying an old gramophone.

"I don't know if this works," explained Mr Van d'Berg. "We haven't played it for ages."

The men crowded round the machine, opened it, cleaned it, and wound it up very gingerly, and *voilà*! it showed signs of life.

The German soldier placed the record gingerly on the turntable, centered the pick-up on the rim of the disc, and waited. It immediately sprang to life. A singer with a decided American voice was singing a song. Although the sound was scratchy, they listened, delighted, and this is what they heard:

Would you like to swing on a star,

Carry moonbeams home in a jar,
And be better off than you are,
Or would you rather be a mule
And all the monkeys aren't in the zoo,
Every day you meet quite a few,
So you see it's all up to you,
You can be better than you are.
You could be swingin' on a star.[13]

It was the first time any of us had heard Bing Crosby. It is not too much to say that after that day, we Mollen youngsters never missed a chance to see his movies when they came to our town. But, delighted though we were, the reality of our situation hit home when the music stopped and the soldier retrieved his record.

"Where did you get that record?" demanded Gerrit.

"I found it. I will tell the truth, since you are good people. I came across a dead American soldier, and I took it from his pack. It was down in the Vosges mountains over Christmas and New Year's and my unit was there during the great battle. It was terrible, with the snow and the cold, and all the slaughter. Eventually, as you probably know, the Allies were reinforced, the skies cleared to allow their air power to take effect, and we were driven back with huge losses. My unit was lucky to get out alive; and we were sent north to reinforce this sector of the front."

---

13 The reader interested in hearing the song has only to search the title on the internet.

The Barn

II.

We hadn't seen Rudy for several weeks when one day—this was in early March, shortly after the shelling began—and we were getting worried, and Gerrit hadn't heard from him or seen him all that time, he turned up without his truck. We were all anxious for his news, and he couldn't answer our questions fast enough. Finally he suggested that he tell his story as it happened, and probably all our questions would be answered. And this is how he told it.

"On my last visit here—it must have been in early January when it was still so bitterly cold—I was really sorry to leave because you had little to eat and I had all the food I needed and I couldn't smuggle any to you.

"I was stopped at the German border as usual, and the guards searched my vehicle, and guess what?—they found a German soldier hiding in the back sound asleep. I was hauled out of my truck and marched into the guardhouse and interrogated. They accused me of scheming with the soldier, and taking a bribe from him, to smuggle him back to Germany. It was, of course, bad enough for a soldier to desert, but if he had help it was doubly bad.

"They kept me and interrogated me constantly for a week, and I stuck to my story. After all, it was the truth. Even if I had wanted to, I couldn't invent a plausible reason why I should want to involve myself in the man's personal grief. He was the enemy! And what could he give me to make it worth my while?

"Of course, they suggested all sorts of 'reasons', or motives, and tried to make me confess. For instance, I was keen to help German soldiers to defect or desert in order to show up their treachery, or to undermine the morale of the others, or to convince them they had lost the war and would spread a sense of defeatism at home.

"They finally gave up and sent me to a prison camp. I was there about four weeks. I was put in solitary confinement, interrogated frequently, put on short rations, and they threatened to take it out on my family if I didn't tell them the truth. I said to them: 'Is that so? If I tell you the truth you won't harm my family?' So I told them the truth. I said: 'I had nothing to do with the German soldier's desertion. That's the truth. **The** truth, not your 'truth'. Go and ask him!"

"The whole matter came to a head when I was able to help an SS officer. His motor bike had broken down and he was anxious to go home. I heard about him and offered to help. When I looked at the machine I saw at once what was wrong with it, and I asked him bluntly: 'If I fix it for you, will you go and find out the truth about that soldier?' He said he would. I had no choice but to trust him, but he was as good as his word. I got his bike working. And a few days later he returned to tell the prison authorities that he had personally spoken to the soldier, who had admitted that I had had nothing to do with it. So they let me go."

We all agreed that was quite a story. But one question lingered in our minds: What happened to the soldier? Rudy never learnt what became of him. But we had to admire his honesty. And we all knew in our hearts what the poor man's fate would have been.

He then told us that he was 'home' to stay, like Gerrit. The cities were becoming so damaged that it was no longer possible to drive vehicles in them to salvage whatever remained to be salvaged. He was actually sent home; but he had to leave his lorry.

"I was half hoping to keep it, for future use!"

"That may yet be possible," added Father somewhat enigmatically.

Later that day, or maybe the next day, Rudy was helping Jan and Bert cut up what little remained of our wood, and because it was so warm they took off their shirts. Perhaps Rudy had forgotten about it, but Jan and Bert could not help noticing great angry welts across Rudy's back and sides.

"What on earth is that, Rudy? What did they do to you?"

"I was hoping you wouldn't see the marks. They flogged me to make me confess. That is their method. And they don't mind whether the confession is the truth or not, so long as they have a pretext to kill or punish a suspect."

III.

"Papers! Schnell! Hurry up!"

Two Germans had burst in, in their usual way. We produced our papers, they examined them suspiciously, as usual, before returning them reluctantly, until they came to Gerrit and Rudy.

"These papers are German identity papers. What are you doing in Holland?"

"We have been released from our work and told to leave."

"Where is your documentation? You must have documentation!"

"No, we don't!" Gerrit protested. "These papers are legitimate and valid for both Germany and for Holland. Here, you can telephone my former employer at this number and he will confirm it."

"Very well," said one of the Germans. "We will do exactly that. And if you are lying we will be back and you will be for the high jump!"

When they turned to leave they almost bumped into Father, who had entered the open door behind them. They started, then shouted in his face:

"Papers!"

He produced his papers from an outside pocket. The Germans looked at them cursorily, and returned them without a further word.

Father followed them out. He came back a couple of minutes later carrying an animal that had been skinned. He handed it to his wife, trying his best to hide his hands. He was unsuccessful.

"Oh, my dear man, what on earth have you done to your hands? They are scratched to pieces!"

"It was this rabbit. It put up quite a fight."

"And I don't have any dressing for your hands. You must wash them right away. I have some baking soda, that's all"

"I have a first aid kit in my bag," said Rudy. "I'll go and get it."

He came back immediately with a small satchel, opened it, and took out a small bottle and a bandage.

"This is iodine.[14] It's going to smart a bit."

Mother took the bottle and gently dabbed father's hands with the liquid, while he did his best not to show his wincing. He spurned the dressing, saying that his hands would heal more quickly if exposed, and, anyway, it would get in the way of work.

---

14 Tincture of iodine was a dark brown liquid with antiseptic properties, and the only such treatment in those days for open cuts and sores. Its application caused a smarting like burning.

IV.

Shortly after these events—and certainly when the taste of the soup, even a German soup, was still a pleasant memory—and between periods of bombardment, we were all summonsed to the mid-day table. Mother, somewhat wryly, but resolutely nevertheless, went the rounds dishing out the lunch. Ria looked down at the 'slop' in her bowl, sniffed at it, withdrew in disgust, and muttered:

"Turnips again. God help us!"

"We all know how you feel, Ria," Father admonished, "but can you do any better?"

"And please watch your language," added Mother.

"It was turnips yesterday. It was turnips last week. It was turnips last month. It will be turnips until I die! Turnip porridge for breakfast; turnip broth for lunch; and turnip stew for supper."

"You're forgetting the turnip pie," teased Jan.

"Not forgetting. Erasing from my mind."

"You're not being fair, Ria. You invoke the name of the Lord, but He has much to do with it; for without this blessing we would have nothing."

"Sometimes—in fact, often—I think the good Lord doesn't know what is going on down here."

"Or doesn't care," added Bert, "which is far worse."

"These turnips," explained Mrs Mollen, "have kept us alive, have kept body and soul together."

"If my soul needs turnips," said Ria, "I am doomed."

"You're not saying much, Ina?" inquired her mother gently.

"I'm so wretched I have nothing to say."

"My poor dear, it will soon be over. Bear up, just a little longer."

"You have gone too far," added Father, in his sternest voice, looking in turn at everyone. "I must remind you all that many untold thousands of people are going through a far worse ordeal than we are. Or not going through it. I am thinking of the poor Jews, and how they have been starved and worked to death."

"It does us good to let off steam now and again," put in Bert, "to say what we really feel."

It was true, and our parents conceded it. They told us later that they had talked together many times, during the past few months especially, and recognized the awful strain they were under—we were all under—and made very considerable allowance for behaviour which they would never normally have indulged. No; 'behaviour' was not an issue: our conduct under stress had always been exemplary. Yes, our speech, our protests, that was all perfectly understandable. And, as Bert had said, 'letting off steam' is a necessary safety valve.

Father's train of thought was broken by the sirens. A new round of artillery bombardments followed immediately; and we all got up and headed for the shelter. Jan, Bert and Ria glanced meaningfully at each other.

"Saved by the shells!"

"At least this time they're friendly shells!"

We made our way to the shelter, hoping and praying that we would not be hit by a stray shell. Perhaps turnips were preferable! We were joined by many other people, residents and refugees, and we all found a place to sit along the benches, with singles and pairs ceding their places so that families could stay together.

There was little to say, and less to do, that hadn't been said and done before. A few people brought out books and tried to read, but without success, for there was not enough light for that, and of course it had been a long time since batteries had been available. There was nothing left, **nothing**. What little conversation started up soon petered out. No, So-and-So hadn't heard from his sister, or aunt, or even mother. There was nothing new under the heavens—or on earth. All one had to do was to wait, wait for the end, and hope.

Then suddenly, unexpectedly, something new did happen! One of the shelterers stood up, noisily drew attention to himself, and, pointing an accusing finger at someone nearby, shouted:

"Who's that there?—why, it's a soldier, a German soldier! What the hell's he doing here?"

The accuser went over to the 'intruder', prodded him bravely in the chest with his finger, and shouted:

"Get out! You're an enemy! You're not wanted in here! Go and face the shelling and let's see what you're made of!"

Everyone was drawn into the scene. Most of us did not know what to say, let alone do, in this strange situation. It was clear that some, perhaps many, were sympathetic towards the soldier. The accused German soldier explained, somewhat timidly:

"We have lost the war. I want no more part in it. Please let me stay."

"No! Out! Get out!"

One man got up and went over to the soldier.

"Now wait a minute! This soldier is giving himself up. We have an obligation to accept his surrender."

"Absolutely not! He's an enemy, a *Boche*! Out with him!"

Then, turning round and appealing to the rest of the people there, he called out:

"You agree with me, don't you? Look how much they have made us suffer for five long years!"

Another man called out from the end of the shelter:

"Yes, I agree. Let him hang!"

A general murmur began to sound in the long inhospitable chamber, but it was difficult to know whether it was a murmur

The Barn

hostile to the German or sympathetic to him. The German took it to be hostile. He stood up.

"All right. I will leave."

"**No, you will not!**"

A booming voice filled the cavern of the shelter; and all of us, wondering, and half intimidated by the authority of the voice, looked toward the source of the voice, and waited.

This new figure advanced toward the soldier, placed a hand on his shoulder, and announced:

"I arrest you in the name of the People, and make you a prisoner of war."

Then, turning to the man who wanted to turn him out, he said:

"You are a mere kid. You have been protected by your family and friends for all these five years, and you don't know what war is. This German soldier has had enough. Can't you see he's an old man? **We have all had enough!** I am going to make sure that one soldier at least returns safely to his own family and survives this bloody war, even if his own rulers did start it."

There was a hushed silence. Then, perhaps not surprisingly, all hundred people in the shelter—save a very few, who looked crestfallen—burst out in long applause.

The man who saved the situation went over to the youngster, put his hand on his shoulder, and said in a voice full of understanding:

"We cannot afford any more hate, son. This man will go home now and help to rebuild a new Germany. Who knows but what comes of a little stone, tossed into an ocean, and sends out ripples..."

At that moment the all-clear sounded, and we all, somewhat relieved on more than one count, made our way out of the shelter and headed for our respective 'homes'. On our way out we saw Father make a point of seeking out the 'arresting citizen' with his captive, and congratulated him on his timely intervention.

"There are times, sir," he replied, "when it seems perfectly clear what has to be done."

"It is a pity that we all do not see things so clearly."

Our family, having returned to the barn, and our unfinished lunch, wasted no time in clearing away the dishes, and boiling up some water to wash them in.

That done, Jan suddenly announced:

"You know, I don't feel hungry any more. On the other hand, despite opinion to the contrary—and he glanced archly in the direction of Ria—we owe much to Mr Turnip."

There was no voice of dissent, only looks all round—part wonder, part amusement—so he felt encouraged to continue.

"In my opinion, the title of 'Mister' does not pay adequate recognition to what we owe him. In the shelter—and before the disturbance with its happy outcome—I began to think of the status we should confer on him. I began to wonder, for example, what Christian name he would have, if he were a real person, and a Christian. And I came to the conclusion that Stephen would be a very suitable name. Yes, it has a noble ring to it. Stephen Turnip. Then I thought: that makes S. Turnip. Why, that is close to being St. Turnip. After all, he has suffered death many times for us. But that is overdoing the 't's', so I've decided to christen him Saint Urnip."

Ria exploded in a fit of indignation mingled with laughter.

"That's ridiculous! I will never pay homage to your St. Urnip!"

"If you are thinking of making a statue of him," warned Mother, "you had better not use one of my real turnips, that's all!"

"It might be a good idea to write to the Pope to apply for regular canonization," added Bert helpfully.

"Don't worry," said Ria. "This saint will have a life-span of all of one month. Then we can go back to our worship of St. Droste.[15] If

---

15 Droste is the name of a popular chocolate.

the Queen ever invites herself to dinner and asks for turnips I shall tell her: 'Sorry, Ma'am, turnips are off!'"

V.

The shelling seemed to go on and on interminably. Every time there was an explosion particularly close to the shelter, the lights, dim as they were, flickered two or three times. Everyone was growing increasingly restive. How much longer would the noise last?—how much longer the hunger, and the uncertainty and insecurity?

Gerrit and Rudy were sitting together and talking, and comparing notes of their experiences. They agreed that, though they, especially Rudy, had been in constant danger in Germany, their perpetual concerns were for their family. Their clothes were getting increasingly worn, they suffered greatly from the cold, especially during those terrible six weeks, and they were losing weight through malnourishment. They felt keenly for Ina and Ria, who at their age should be putting on weight and getting a healthy diet. They felt guilty for being well fed themselves, and impotent to help. The one great blessing was—and we have mentioned it before—that through all our ordeals no one was ever sick for a single day.

"Amazingly, and thankfully," said Gerrit, "their morale seems as high as ever. They just refuse to give in, and are determined to outlast those damned Germans."

"You know," said Rudy, "I almost hate to admit it, but you have to hand it to the Germans as well. Their cities have been reduced to rubble and the civilians keep going as best they can—just as the Londoners did in what they called their 'Blitz'.[16]

"Yes, but the London 'Blitz' only lasted for six months. The German armies, while knowing what is happening at home, do not give an inch and fight like tigers. And that is not only on the Eastern front against the Russians, but on two other fronts as well."

"It makes you wonder whether these bombing campaigns are producing the results the air forces hope for. All I knew was what I saw happening on the ground. Did you get other kinds of information about the war from Mr Oldenkott?"

"Yes, although limited. He had to be careful what he said—not only to me but to anyone. For example, one interesting thing he said was he wondered who was in charge of the Allied campaign—by which he meant, who selected the targets, and how they determined their priorities."

"And perhaps how they assessed the results of the bombing, if they did assess them?"

"Yes; but their only means was by photography. But photography, while it showed the results of physical damage to houses, for example, could not assess morale."

"And we could have given them some information about—that if they had asked us!"

"But you would think they could infer that from the *Wehrmacht*'s fighting spirit."

At this moment the shelling became closer and louder and more intense, and made talking impossible. When it died down and a relative silence returned, Rudy said he was fed up with the shelter and decided to go back to the barn and see whether he could get any news from the wireless.

---

16   It is worth noting that the 'Blitz' lasted for only eight months, mostly against London, whereas the bombing of Germany's cities went on with increasing destruction for four years, from 1942 to 1945.

The silence went on, and on, for a good half-hour; even so sleep was impossible. Bert said he was wide awake, and itching to know what was going on, and suggested to Ria that they go and look.

"You know that tower outside? I've been up it a few times recently, and you get a marvellous view all round, and with the shelling getting closer ..."

"Yes, a good idea. I'm game."

Our parents looked at each other, worriedly, but figuratively shrugging their shoulders. They could no longer prevent us now.

As Bert and Ria got up and started for the door of the shelter, a man stood up and asked if he could go with them. The three of them left, and, hardly had they got to the middle of the road when there was a shattering explosion, and a brilliant flash of light which half blinded them. Bert and Ria took to their heels to get to out of the road and hopefully to safety. They reached a building, turned with their backs pressed against it to look back, and realized their neighbour was no long with them. Then they saw him—he was lying in the middle of the road. Bert and Ria went over cautiously to look at him. He was covered in blood, and quite motionless. They returned to the shelter and told what had happened. Gerrit got up and went outside. He returned almost immediately, and, standing at the entrance, called out:

"The man looks dead. I need someone to help me to move him off the road."

He looked around, and no one volunteered. Finally, one man stood up and said he would help. It was the same German soldier. The two men left. They found a ladder and took him to the hospital nearby, where he died. He had been hit by a large piece of shrapnel in the stomach.

The shelling started up again, and got louder and louder, until we thought it would come right into our shelter. Then, slowly and gradually, it died away, and seemed to recede into the distance. An hour passed, perhaps two, and all was still and eerily silent.

The Barn

There was still no sleep for anyone that night, for now a mood of expectancy hung in the air.

We were all huddled in our blankets. It must have been about three o'clock in the night of April 1-2. For a time it seemed that the sound of battle began again, and grew louder; it reached what must have been a *crescendo*; and then gradually faded away again, like a dying sigh.

The silence was followed by what sounded to us all in the shelter the heavy noise of clanking and rattling. It was like the German tanks of 1940, but not so menacing. There was another difference this time: there was no shouting. The varied noises died away, and silence descended on the scene, a welcome silence that seemed to invite sleep. But no, not this night of all nights!

The next moment all eyes were turned towards a light descending the stairs, and coming closer. It entered our shelter, and there we saw a tall officer, in the uniform of an Allied soldier. He saluted, and said in English:

"The Germans have gone. You are safe now. You may leave the shelter."

Many of us understood what he said; many others didn't—until a woman at the end got up and shouted:

"Wij zijn vrij! We are free!"

The outburst of cheering and shouting, amid laughter and crying, was spontaneous and deafening. We all stood up, and looked at each other, staring, not knowing whether to believe it, or how to behave! Slowly this incredible news seeped through to us, and we believed.

Those of us who understood what the officer had said were impressed by his manner. In contrast to the Germans, with their harsh guttural language shouted in your face, the soldier's speech, brief though his words were, was calm and almost gentle, the voice of reason and civilization. It was music to our ears.

We all started slowly, and in orderly fashion, to make our way out of the shelter to the outside. At the end of the road we saw the last of what must have been a long file of Allied tanks turn the corner and disappear.

We walked about, freely, still hardly daring to believe the good fortune that had descended upon us like a balming and blessed rain. We didn't want to leave: we wanted so keenly to savour this delirious moment. But finally people began to drift away, and head back to their homes and lodgings; and we did the same.

It must have been about seven o'clock before we got back to our barn. And no sooner had we returned than Mother and Father announced that we were to go to church. We walked along the road to St Martinus Church in Didam, scarcely noticing whether we were tired or not. The church was packed full, even more so than usual. And even more than usually, most people paid rapt attention to the sermon, for the good Father took as his theme the text of Isaiah 61, 1:

The spirit of the Lord God is upon me
because the Lord has anointed me;
he has sent me to bring good news to the humble,
to bind up the broken-hearted
to proclaim liberty to captives
and release to those in prison.

ST. MARTINUS CHURCH

We could not help but notice several soldiers in the church. But what astounded us was to see a German soldier as well. After the service he took his time to leave. We waited. When the German soldier did appear he was accompanied by two of 'our' soldiers. They stopped, and appeared to start talking. Father said he was not going to miss this, and discreetly moved close enough to hear what they were saying. We followed, and tried to give every sign of lingering for its own sake, rather than for eavesdropping. This is what Father told us that he heard:

".... yes, I have deserted from the German Army. I am old.... like that gentleman there (he was indicating Father) and we have lost the war, and to go on throwing good young lives away, when they will be needed for rebuilding Germany after the war, why, it's plain madness."

"But then Hitler is either mad or evil. Or both. Why did you Germans follow him so slavishly?"

"Well, at the beginning—and I remember those years well. I was forty-six then, when the *Fürher* came to power. He performed wonders, miracles! Everyone believed in him! There was nothing he could not accomplish. Above all, he made us feel a pride in ourselves, in being German, after the humiliation of the First World War. And the way we just took over the Sudetenland, and Austria, and then Czechoslovakia, without a murmur from all those weak democracies, especially France, and Great Britain with her mighty Empire! So that later, when rumours began to spread about pogroms and the Jewish question, well, either we didn't believe it or it was just Jewish propaganda. Of course, by then, it was too late."

"But there were some Germans who saw from the beginning what Hitler was up to, and they opposed him."

"Yes, that is so, but they were quickly eliminated, and we didn't hear anything more from or about them."

"Tell me, do you have chaplains in the German Army?—you know, priests and other church ministers?"

"Oh, yes!"

"And how did they justify their ministry? Did they pray for victory, for the success of German arms, for Hitler's justification in the eyes of God?"

"Not exactly in those terms. I seem to think that they prayed more for the safety of the Church, and for the souls of the Germans killed in battle. And your clergymen?—I suppose they claimed that God was on your side?"

"It was not exactly like that. For us, it was to strive to be on God's side."

It was at this point that the two Allied soldiers moved off, taking the German with them as prisoner.[17]

---

17 Doetinchem was liberated by units of the Fort Garry Horse armoured regiment of Winnipeg. Later that day and following the mopping-up of snipers and consolidation of the operation was carried out by the Canadian infantry regiment, the Black Watch.

VI.

When we got back to our barn—it was ten or eleven o'clock by now—we were all very restless. It was difficult to know what to do. We wanted desperately to go back to Arnhem, and home; but we had no news, and didn't know how long we were going to have to remain in the barn. Moreover, everything was so quiet and peaceful. Soldiers were marching past, but we hardly heard them—no stamping, no shouting, no noise. Just a quiet and peaceful liberation.

Rudy, who had been out reconnoitering the situation, came back just then accompanied by an Army officer and a sergeant. They wore "Canada" flashes on their shoulders. The officer goes up to our parents and salutes. The family gather round. Church bells are heard faintly but distinctly in the distance. The officer introduces himself:

"I am Captain Northrop, and my NCO is Sergeant Frazer. It may be a superfluous question, but I wish to know what you need immediately."

"There is nothing we do not need," answered Mother..

"We need to go home," added Ina.

"Where do you live?"

"We live in Arnhem."

"Then I'm very much afraid it will not be possible for you to go back to your home in under two or three weeks. There is much work to be done in Arnhem before then. The city has been heavily damaged in the fighting. In the meantime you may collect food and clothing at the Town Hall from tomorrow. And on Wednesday we hope to have any medical services you may need."

"Is the war over—finally over?" asked Ria, almost pleadingly, as if needing to be reassured once again.

"For you and your family it is, Miss."

Sergeant Frazer then spoke for the first time:

"We have a lot of fighting still ahead of us. The Germans haven't surrendered yet, and if we know them there's a lot of fight left in them."

As if to corroborate his words, the sound of renewed shelling in the distance penetrated into their newly safe abode. At the sound of the renewed barrage Ina put her hands over her ears; and Ria burst out passionately:

"Why does there have to be war?"

"I don't know, Miss. I wish I did. All I know is that there is good in the world and there is evil in the world. And the good has to defend itself. Now you are happy we are here?"

"Oh, yes! You are our deliverers, our saviours, the enders of the war."

"I do not like war either, Miss. But I have no patience with people who would not raise a finger to expose or fight evil, or to defend their families. And sometimes it amounts to the same thing. For the same reason. And you may not understand this, but at some moments in history it is probable that the world would be a worse place if there not war."

"You are right, I do not understand why war can be better than no war."

Sergeant Frazer stepped forward and reminded his Captain that they had many other refugee families to attend to. And Father thanked the two soldiers for their help and compassion. But Captain Northrop had one more thing to say. And he addressed us thus:

"Let me put it this way. If we abolish the police, will we do away with crime? Will getting rid of firemen prevent fires? Please

The Barn **167**

don't misunderstand me. You are brave people and you have done everything you could, which is to survive. I could tell you stories of your countrymen's bravery and sacrifice for others..."

"I am sure that it will all come out after the war... and the treachery."

"I feel," said Ina, "as if I had been encased in ice for the last six months. Now for the first time I feel a breath of warmth float over me."

"May you be warm for the rest of your life, Miss. We must now see to other families. God bless you all."

Captain Northrop saluted and made for the door with his sergeant. As they left they were accompanied by both Gerrit and Rudy, who overheard what they said to each other, perhaps as if they wanted to be overheard:

"Can we even guess what they have been through, these brave people? They look so thin."

"Thin, yes, but not worn," replied his sergeant. "It is a marvel that they have come through at all, in view of the tales and rumours we heard before getting here."

"The marvel is, with their humanity intact, in view of the Nazi brutality they have contended with for five long years." Then, as if communing with himself: "The old Roman said it well: *Magna est enim vis humanitatis: multum valet communio sanguinis.*"

"Meaning, sir?"

"Strong is the bond of our common humanity; firm are the ties of family."

* * *

We, our family, made up as we were of parents and their 'children', had to survive as a family or not at all. For our part, we the youngsters, give infinite credit to our parents for looking after us, and for setting such a stalwart example to us. They hadn't finished.

"Old as we are, we will start again and rebuild everything from scratch."

"After all, everyone will be in the same boat."

"That is true," said Gerrit. "And we are young."

The church bells rang out again, as if in sign both of remembrance and summons.

"Come, children, it is Easter Sunday. We must get ready for church."

"But, Mother," expostulated Ria, "we have been to church already today. Today we have to go and cheer the soldiers, who liberated us. They are still marching by. They are so different from ...." she did not finish her thought, it was so painful.

"I am sure you are right, my dear. But they will still be here after Church...."

"...and the Lord will be here even longer, if ...."

"Ria, we do our duty before our pleasure. Our duty is to give thanks for our deliverance."

"Oh, Papa! Will you never take my side?" exclaimed Ria, stamping her foot petulantly. "I have done more than my duty for five horrible years, and I don't see that the Lord has done his. After five years of this duty, I want some pleasure **now.**"

"Ria, you heard what the officer said. We will be here another two or three weeks. You will see plenty of soldiers."

The church bells rang out louder, as if in part in celebration, and in part in a call to service.

They were on the point of leaving when Father stopped suddenly, as if trying to remember something important.

"Dear me, I was almost forgetting."

He fumbles in his pocket and finally produces a gold ring. He replaces it on his wife's finger, saying:

"I didn't need it after all. That ca.... that rabbit was a bit wild, but it was free. That's what hurt most."

"You have been an unshakeable tower of strength, my dear."

The Barn

"The head is useless without its heart and soul. And would we have survived without the children?"

"Would it have been worth surviving without them?"

"Mama!" exclaimed Ina. "Where is all your jewellery? You mean you have sold it all?"

"Not 'sold' exactly, dear. Exchanged for food. You can't eat pearls, you know."

"You mean to say you have none of your jewels left?"

"You are worth more to me than all the jewels of Europe."

"Oh, Mama!" cried Ina, as she threw herself into her mother's arms.

* * *

It seemed to this good family that the church bells get louder, more insistent. The family make their way out, and head once again down the road towards the church. And Ria's head is turned the other way, looking wistfully in the direction taken by their Canadian liberators.

POSTLUDE

Our family were made much more comfortable during the next few weeks, thanks to new clothes and blankets, and above all of food—food of a variety and quality that they had not seen for what seemed like an age

Their newly restored freedom was a blessing which they had not adequately prized before: they had taken it so much for granted. Never again! People who do not know freedom—the freedom to come and go as they please, and to say what they like, and even to offend the authorities—strive mightily, and run huge risks, often at the cost of their lives, to regain it. They thought, these good people, that they will never be tempted to barter it away, shall we say? in exchange for promised safety or security. No, never would they sell their birthright for a mess of potage of lentils!

Above all, what they savoured in those days was the peace and quiet. They could not fathom the mentality of the Germans who had to go round making a noise wherever they went and whatever they did. It is almost as if they were afraid of silence, and were somehow reassured by noise. These Canadian soldiers were gentlemen!—they moved and spoke and behaved so calmly and quietly.

Over the following two or three weeks the Canadian soldiers moved on and some British soldiers moved in to replace them. On one day Ina and Ria were out walking when they passed by a few Army trucks parked beside the road. The soldiers were cooking a meal. Hardly had the two girls passed when Ria stopped, sniffed the air, and said to her sister:

"Ina, do you smell that? It's frying bacon! Have you ever smelled anything so heavenly?"

"Come on, Ria! We mustn't stop!"

"Why not? I'm going to stand close to them ...."

"You can't do that! Come on!" and she started pulling Ria by the arm.

"Just watch me!" as she pulled free of Ina's grip.

The soldiers looked up and saw Ria, who was looking longingly in their direction.

"Would you like some? Do you know what we're cooking?"

"No; but it smells heavenly."

"It is! We're having eggs and bacon. Would you like some?"

Ria looked round. Ina was gone. And Ria had her heavenly meal.

"Where on earth do you get eggs?" she asked. "Did you bring chickens with you?"

"Gawd bless you, no, miss!" replied one soldier. "It's the Yanks what supply us. Maybe the've brought some 'ens wiv 'em. They've got everything, them Yanks 'ave."

* * *

It was 'Yanks' who came after the British, passing through our sector on the way to the front, which was driving farther and farther to the east. There was still heard a bit of distant artillery fire, but day by day it receded towards the east.

One day an American convoy passed through and stopped to make lunch at the roadside. Ria and her sister and brothers were out and about and all over the place, singly and in pairs, savouring the fruits of freedom, and stopping to chat to anyone and everyone. Ria happened upon this convoy; and as she was walking past the trucks lined up beside the road, she glanced up at one of the drivers, and was met by one of the broadest grins of the whitest teeth—in the blackest face—she had ever seen.

This driver leant out of his cab, smiled 'from ear to ear', and beckoned her over. Overcoming a lingering doubt, Ria approached cautiously, though secure in the knowledge that it is broad daylight and there are masses of troops about, she approached close to the driver, who handed her a number of items:

"This," he said, handing her some cigarettes, "is for Papa. This (it was chocolate) is for Mama. And this is for you."

Ria took the proffered presents, thanked the soldier, and headed off for home. His present for Ria was a packet of chewing-gum. She was to chew and re-chew that gum for weeks after, being sure to replace a chewed piece back in its wrapper until needed again.

* * *

There was not only peace and orderliness in the wake of the German withdrawal: there were also, unhappily, scenes of disorder and controversy.

Inevitably, and for reasons that will be understood by everyone who is not an unbending moralist, some Dutch girls were tempted to accept an invitation to go out with a German soldier. Some of them simply wanted to "have a good time", or to enjoy material things not available to others. Others, however, but very, very few, were seen, or suspected, to have been active collaborators, in the sense that they put their own pleasure or survival above all other considerations. For those girls and women, there would be no forgiveness and no pity.

They were known, and they were rounded up. And they were maltreated. The first batch of such women were paraded in the main square just a few days after the Liberation. But not anyone was authorized to do it. They were sought out, questioned, and convicted only by men who had worked with the Resistance, at the risk of their lives, and of the safety of their families. These men wore red arm-bands, so they would be recognized. And accorded very great respect for what they had done during the war.

On this morning, twenty or so men of the Resistance herded into the square a group of a dozen women. Awaiting them was a row of plain wooden chairs. The women were pushed into the chairs, with their feet bound, and their hands bound behind their backs. Behind each of the women stood two men. The men were equipped with scissors and clippers. And they set to work with a will, shearing the women's heads, and ridding them of their "crowning glory", until they looked freakish. Then they were released, to be shunned, ridiculed and scorned by all.

On the following morning, the same scene was re-enacted: more women were rounded up and shaved in public. Towards the end of this punishment, Bert and Ria chanced to arrive at the square in time to witness their release. One girl in particular attracted their attention. Ria pointed her out to Bert:

"Isn't that Nietje? Nietje Jansen? They all look so different without their hair, but I could swear that's her."

"It certainly looks like her."

Ria called out: "Nietje!"

The girl turned round and looked. She recognized Ria, and started crying.

"This is not right! Nietje never went out with German soldiers."

"That's right! And look at that fellow with the arm-band smirking! That's Jan-Piet. He was never in the Resistance. Let's go and find out what's going on."

SHAVING A GIRL'S HEAD

They found the Chief in charge of the Proceedings, and he explained the case to them. It turned out that Jan-Piet was acting out of spite. Quite simply, Nietje had refused on many occasions to go out with him and he was getting his own back. He was arrested, charged, prosecuted, tried, convicted—all according to our ancient customs and traditions of law, and sentenced to a salutary term in prison, to enable him to reflect on his vileness.

* * *

It was now late April, and Spring was in the air. The air was warming, it was a delight to go walking in the countryside again. The trees and shrubs were putting out new green leaf, there were flowers coming into blossom, and birds were singing again. We felt little wonder that poets of all ages celebrated Spring as a season of rebirth and rejuvenation.

So it was that an officer reported to our parents and asked us to be ready to move back to Arnhem the following morning. We said our grateful goodbyes to our hosts and benefactors, and prepared for our departure.

An Army truck arrived promptly at eight o'clock the following morning, and we all boarded it, and found ourselves sitting on two benches running along each side of the vehicle and facing each other. We were on the point of moving off when suddenly Father calls out:

"Wait! I've forgotten something."

We all look at each other, wondering what he could have possibly forgotten—after all, we were taking almost nothing back with us because nothing was worth taking—when he reappears clutching an object as if it was the Crown jewels. He climbed back into the truck, gave the sign to leave, and resumed his seat beside Mother and, with a broad grin of triumph, showed us his radio.

"Our lifeline. We are going to need this back home."

The journey back to Arnhem, which had taken us three days in the other direction seven months before, took us this time somewhat less than three hours. We were deposited on our doorstep, and we all looked forward to what promised to be a new, and different, and better, life.

Our house looked little changed, on the outside. We had heard that the city of Arnhem had suffered very considerable damage and destruction, especially in the central parts of the city, during the second battle of Arnhem; but we were some way outside the centre, on the road to Zevenaar.

We looked up and down the street. How familiar it seemed! And how welcoming. To be sure, there was damage; the whole area looked a bit like a deserted island. But it was home.

We tried the front door, tentatively. It opened. We went in, one by one, wondering what we would find. We were not exactly surprised. It was empty. More than that: it was a shell. It had been gutted. Everything movable had been taken, and much that was fixed had been wrenched from the walls.

It was not unlike our barn, at the beginning. But there were differences. This was our home, and it was going to be permanent, and we were surrounded by our own kith and kin.

And there was another thing. We were going to have to start and to build from nothing, and we were all in the same boat.

Bit by bit, hour by hour and day by day, and week by week, we set about restoring our home, our business, and our lives.

We discovered that the military had already created and handed over the administration of the city to a civic authority. They had already restored electric power; and telephone service would be ready within the month.

Some things we would never forget, or get over. One example: Although we were all fluent in the German language, whenever thereafter we heard a German voice we would flinch, and wince, and almost cringe, at the sounds made by a people we loathed and despised and scorned with such intensity of feeling.

We found it impossible to understand how a cultured people like the Germans could fall for the racist ranting of a pathological maniac like Hitler; or how so few of the people could show the courage to oppose, by word or deed, the horrors unleashed on an unsuspecting and undeserving mankind.

It is no exaggeration to say that many, many years passed before we, the Dutch people, could hear the German language again without an instinctive recoiling within ourselves, and before we could again accept them as equal members of the human race.

If it is possible for good to come out of evil—and even to express the event in those terms may be wrong—we can take a measure of satisfaction in witnessing the transformation of Germany into a prosperous and dynamic democracy, and in looking at ourselves with a small measure of modest pride in the knowledge that the German people owe to us, by our resistance, an acknowledgement of the role we played in that transformation.

Appendix A

EVACUATION ORDER.

While the drama of Putten took place in the north of the Veluwe, the Germans staged another tragedy south of the forest. J. Douwenga, a schoolteacher in Wageningen, woke up on Sunday, 1 October, to hear a strange sound he could at first not identify. 'It was like the slow shuffle of thousands of feet, but there was no sound of voices.' He opened the curtains. 'We looked; we just looked. What I saw was so tragic, so terribly sad, that it overwhelmed us completely. My wife could not bear it any longer and burst out into tears. An endless stream of refugees . . . walked past in the pouring rain. . . . They were soaked to the skin, and silent. Yellow leaves were falling from the trees.'

The Germans had ordered the evacuation of a series of places which had been badly hit during the Battle of Arnhem. Their populations had for ten days lived in their cellars and had hoped that, now the fighting was over, they would have some peace and quiet. The order to depart came as a shattering blow, but dulled by recent events they began to march—with nowhere to go.

Arnhem itself had been hit by the same fate a week before. The town looked like a surrealist nightmare—it was a total ruin. On 23 September the last convulsions of the battle that had given so much hope to the Dutch were taking place on the Oosterbeek perimeter, but in Arnhem the population had surfaced and were trying to repair the roofs over their heads. Then at four o'clock that Saturday afternoon Dr J. N. van der Does, a surgeon and head of the provincial Red Cross, was summoned to SS Headquarters. An officer, pointing to a map on the wall, told Van der Does without ceremony that everybody living south of the railway track that divided the town in half must leave before eight o'clock that evening. The rest had to follow within twenty-four hours. Van der Does's protests were cut short. 'If any man, woman or child is found in town after tomorrow night,' the officer snapped, 'it will be the worse for them. Save your breath and empty your town.'

To Van der Does, it seemed an impossible task. How to evacuate 100,000 people within thirty-six hours or less? Arnhem's Nazi mayor and police chief had disappeared on Mad Tuesday and the town elders had 'dived', fearing reprisals after a vital railway viaduct had been sabotaged. The only man who pretended to have some authority was former shoe seller A. F. Hollaar, self-styled deputy mayor, who approved the German decision. A last effort by some prominent Arnhemmers to change the mind of the Germans failed. 'No stone will be left upon another,' Major Peters, the second-in-command in the German HQ, told them, and when Van der Does received written instructions later that day the orderly warned him that a 'blanket of bombs' would be laid over Arnhem if he disobeyed.

It was too late at night to order the departure, and only next morning the horrified Arnhemmers received the fatal message, printed on a piece of grey paper and signed by Hollaar as 'Police President of Arnhem'. Van der Does advised them to carry only the barest necessities with them.

*   *   *

Women cried and men cursed, but everybody started to pack obediently and to load their few possessions on prams, hand-carts and bikes. On Sunday afternoon the exodus started. Most of the evacuees went in the direction of Apeldoorn, thirty kilometres away. The hilly road was overcrowded, the rain was falling and the only sound one could hear was that of crying children 'tied on top of the luggage, cold and hungry.' The autumn nights were already cold, and no one had anywhere to go. 'It made no difference if one was rich or poor,' someone wrote. 'They all marched slowly on with the same miserable belongings, like outcasts.'

That first night, most of the refugees found a roof in one of the surrounding villages, and many of them stayed the whole winter on the Veluwe. Others travelled on to the north and passed the winter in Friesland. The few who tried to go back to Arnhem found the town sealed off by patrolling Germans, who threatened to shoot if they ever tried again to enter.

It is still a big mystery who ordered the evacuation. The local German commander never knew about it and Major Peters disappeared—seen for the last time in a car full of loot. For Van der Does it was by then too late to revoke the order. The exodus had been completed—and three thousand Arnhemmers would not live to see their town again.

(Source : H. Van der Zee, *The Hunger Winter*, pp. 47-48.)

Appendix B

AFTER TANK COMBAT, FARM LIFE NOT THE SAME.

Two people sharing a table in a Victoria coffee shop in 2010 discover they have a connection to the Second World War. 'She' survived the Hunger Winter in Holland. 'He' survived the Second World War in a Sherman tank. 'She' was Rika Dixon (formerly Moerkes); 'he' was Jim Vanyo whose story this is chiefly.

"We got to sharing a few stories," said Rika, who moved to Canada in 1956 and retired with her husband Jack to Saanich 20 years ago. They found they had a lot to talk about. Jim, who was a tank signalman (radio operator) with the Fort Garry Horse regiment, was passing through the Netherlands town of Doetinchem on April 1, 1945. The arrival of the Canadian army meant liberation and the end of Nazi occupation. Since

September of 1944, Rika and her family had been living in a barn just outside Doetinchem. They had been evacuated from their home in Arnhem, 20 kilometres to the west. Rika remembers eating a turnip-heavy diet. The turnips were used as cattle feed but there were no more cattle and there was little else to eat. Summer was coming but it didn't matter, she said. The Nazi occupation wouldn't allow them to work the fields. "A lot of people died of hunger. Sometimes we would walk 20 kilometers for a glass of milk or two potatoes."

Jim's story of how he came to be a radio operator in a tank that fought its way through the Netherlands went back to his days on the farm in Middle Lake, Sask., in 1942. "Soon after I turned 18 I got on my bicycle and pedaled it, partly broken, 20 miles to Cudworth, the next town," Jim said. "I sold my bike and bought a bus ticket to Saskatoon. I wanted to join the navy, all the boys my age did, but the navy wasn't ready for me and said I'd have to wait at home for another month. I said, 'No way in hell I'm going back to farming'."

So he joined the army, which took him right away. "My brother was in the tanks so I told them, 'Tanks or nothing,' and they said 'No problem'." Jim trained as a gunner but by the time he arrived at Juno Beach on D-Day 1944, he was a wireless radio operator. "Actually, our first tank never made it ashore." Before it could launch from the landing craft the whole unit sank, one of many casualties suffered during the epic landing. With the tank went some of Vanyo's personal belongings and the crew's prized bottle of moonshine. "I got in another tank on Day 2 and we made a night push to get as far inland from the beach as possible to attain our objective."

For seven months, Jim was in the same Sherman tank. And, for the most part, he had the same crew. He never knew it until later in the war but, because of his voice, Jim had become the 'go-to' radio operator for the Garry's (as the Regiment's members were called) meant our tank was often the one designated to go into a field. "We didn't figure that out for a while," he said. Modest and shy to talk about himself, Jim says he never thought much of it but in retrospect, his long passion for radio started then. Once, when I was standing with some of the Garry's men and our commanding officer, Lt. Colonel A. Morton, was there. He said, 'All of you pay attention to how (Vanyo speaks). This is how you should talk'."

CORPORAL JIM VANYO
AND HIS TANK CREW BELGIUM 1944

Jim eventually became the regimental wireless control operator. After V-E Day many of the Garry's returned to Doetinchem and helped the citizens re-establish their town. The regiment built Canada Park with one of their Sherman tanks as the centrepiece. It was refurbished by the city in 1994, on the 50th anniversary of D-Day. Since the war's end, Vanyo has built a collection of 250 classic radios. He even owned a radio shop in Lake Cowichan for a few years. His squadron's journey from D-Day (June 6, 1944) to V-E Day (May 8, 1945) is chronicled in the Fort Garry Horse

Regiment museum publication "Vanguard, The Fort Garry Horse in the Second World War."

(By Travis Paterson, "Victoria News", November 10, 2010. Edited by Jack Dixon.)

Recognition. Unable to attend many of the commemorations happening around the country, Jim recently received letters from Prime Minister Stephen Harper, the Ministry of Veterans' affairs, and a medal from the Dutch government.

Jim died, of natural causes, on 23 October 2011.

JIM VANYO AND RIKA DIXON
AT THE COFFEE SHOP

About the Author

Jack Dixon was born in Kent, England, in 1924. At 16, he joined the Royal Air Force as an apprentice and trained as an armourer. He chose aircrew later and earned his pilot's 'wings' in 1945, just as the war in the Far East ended. Obtaining his release in 1948, Jack studied in France for a year before going to Merton College Oxford, where he graduated with an Honours degree in Modern Languages. After emigrating to Canada in 1952, Jack served for 5 years in the R.C.A.F. before deciding on an academic career. He met his wife Rika in Vancouver in 1959 and they moved to Winnipeg where Jack took up a position at then United College (later the University of Winnipeg) as a lecturer in French. Jack took his PhD at Stanford and taught at Winnipeg until his retirement in 1991. Jack and Rika have lived happily in Victoria, British Columbia, since then. They have travelled widely in many parts of the world. Jack continues to write, having published four books, the last two being *Dowding and Churchill: The Dark Side of the Battle of Britain*, and *The Literary Culture of France*.

CPSIA information can be obtained
at www.ICGtesting.com
Printed in the USA
LVOW11s1857210317
527964LV00004B/967/P